Wavescape

Wavescape

Portraits of the Planet's Best Surf Spots

Chris Towery and Matt Pruett

BARRON'S

First edition for the United States and Canada published in 2002 by
Barron's Educational Series, Inc.

Produced by PRC Publishing Ltd.,
64 Brewery Road, London N7 9NT

A member of **Chrysalis** Books plc

© 2002 PRC Publishing Ltd.

All inquiries should be addressed to:
Barron's Educational Series, Inc.
250 Wireless Boulevard
Hauppauge, NY 11788
http://www.barronseduc.com

International Standard Book No. 0-7641-5538-5

Library of Congress Catalog Card No. 2001099624

Printed in Taiwan

9 8 7 6 5 4 3 2 1

Frontispiece: *The tube ride. A relatively modern maneuver with timeless style.*

ACKNOWLEDGMENTS

The publisher wishes to thank the photographers and libraries who kindly supplied the photography
   for this book, as follows:

Bruce Chrisner/Oceanview Photography for pages 2, 102 (bottom) and 103;
Tom Dugan/© www.easternsurf.com for pages 6-7, 16-17, 22, 24-25, 26 (top and bottom), 27, 36
   (top and bottom), 37, 39, 74-75, 80, 81, 82 (top), 83, 84, 85 (main and inset), 90 (top and bottom),
   91, 92-93,
94-95, 96, 97 (main and inset), 98, 99, 100, 110, 118-119, 124 (top), 130, 131, 134 , 135 (main and
   inset), 143 (main and left) and 144;
Alex Williams for pages 8 (top), 10 (left), 15, 34, 35 (top and bottom), 40 (left), 66, 68, 76, 77, 112 and
   113;
© Dick Meseroll/© www.easternsurf.com for pages 8 (bottom), 10-11 (main), 12, 13 (top), 14, 20, 21,
   23, 82 (bottom), 102 (top), 108, 109, 111 (main and inset), 116 (top and bottom), 117, 124 (bot-
   tom), 125, 126, 127, 132, 133 (main and inset), 145 (left and right), 146 (left and right) and 147;
© Barry Tuck for pages 9, 18, 19, 46, 47 (main), 48, 49 (main), 50, 51, 158 and 159;
© Pete Frieden Photography for pages 28, 29, 30, 32, 41, 49 (inset), 61 (main), 67, 69, 73, 88, 89,
   150 and 151;
© Chris Van Lennep for pages 32, 33, 42-43 and 47 (inset);
© Grant Ellis for pages 38, 138-139 and 140-141;
John Steinhorst for pages 44 and 45 (main and inset);
© Bosko for pages 56-57;
© Bill Morris for pages 58-59, 63 and 129;
Mike Findlay for pages 60 and 61 (inset);
© Joli for pages 52, 53, 54-55, 62, 72, 101, 148-149, 152, 153, 154, 155, 156 and 157;
© Jeff Flindt for pages 64 and 65;
© John S Callahan for pages 70-71 and 122;
Jeff Divine for pages 78, 79 and 106-107;
© Scott Winer for pages 86, 87, 104, 105 (main and bottom left), 120 and 121;
Dave Nelson for page 114;
Kookson for page 115;
Zof for page 123;
© Reuben Pina for page 128;
Sharp for page 136;
© Klein for page 137;
© Rucki for page 142;

See jacket for cover photo credits.

Contents

INTRODUCTION

Surfers are nomadic by nature. From the very first Polynesian waveriders island-hopping their way through the Pacific to today's bankrolled boat trips through the Mentawais Islands, our tribe has forever been wandering the planet in search of surf. Because the very medium upon which we ride is an ever-flowing and constantly changing liquid, surfers are forced to stay in tune with the earth's fluctuating patterns of wind, tide, and swell, constantly seeking out new destinations where these mutable elements come together best. Like ancient hunters following herds of prey across the continents, this quest has led us to the ends of the earth and back again.

Right: *After taking that first drop, surfers often become hooked. Jeremy Saukel savoring the rush at Indicas.*

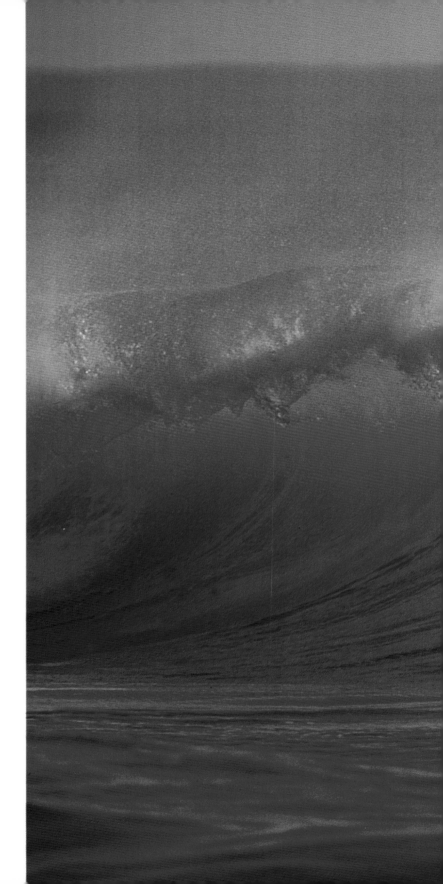

Traversing the planet en masse since the advent of foam and fiberglass, surfers have followed the Earth's violent storm energy from ocean to ocean, continent to continent, island to island, and coast to coast, all the while colonizing the globe's loneliest outposts with the very spirit of our stoke. From the beginning, our sport has been one of history's greatest agents for cultural exchange. From Australia to the Andamans, Costa Rica to Canada, Ireland to Indonesia, Peru to Portugal, New York to New Zealand, we've interacted with almost every population near a surfable coastline. And like religious missionaries, we've shared and passed along our passion to legions of indigenous people. The sheer, unbridled

pleasure of riding waves is now enjoyed on a global level, and our tribe inhabits every continent on Earth except Antarctica. What other group of sportsmen can claim such a far-reaching impact?

Wavescape tours this global surfing village and documents many of our planet's most epic surfbreaks. From spots discovered ages ago to places uncovered only in the last few years, this book follows surfers' footprints across the earth and spotlights a sample of the lineups that have fueled our wanderlust. However, our migrations haven't been only for waves, and to understand how surfing has evolved into such a worldwide phenomenon, it's first necessary to look back over history to examine the other catalysts that have sparked our sport's

Above: *Big-game hunters flock to Africa seeking many of its exotic species of animals, but surfers hit the continent looking for a different type of quarry. Nigel Gibb with watery prey in his cross-hairs at Durban.*

Above Left: *You'll find our tribe inhabiting some of the most unlikely places. Shawn Skilton floats one in southwest England.*

Left: *While it doesn't get the biggest waves in the world, Florida has produced some of the greatest surfers on the planet. Justin Ellingham at First Peak, Sebastian Inlet—the home of two world champions.*

burgeoning growth. It's been a long time since that first Polynesian rose unsteadily to his feet, but from that moment on, it's been one hell of a wild ride.

Origins

This amazing journey began around 4,000 years ago when the seeds of surfriding were first planted by ancient Southeast Asian seafarers migrating westward into Polynesia. This far-reaching chain of South Pacific islands was colonized by these early travelers, who, due to their intimate involvement with the sea, were accomplished watermen. As these people crossed from island to island in their twin-hulled canoes, they learned to ride the ocean's swells. From coasting ashore with the waves in their boats, they eventually took to the water using more fitting surfriding vehicles. Employing short bodyboard-like planks known as "paipos," the early Polynesians had discovered surfing, though the stand-up version didn't get up and trimming until the ocean voyagers headed north to Hawaii around 400 A.D. Once there, the surfcraft grew longer and longer, and, as the boards gained more stability, people began to rise to their feet. With the advent of the lengthier stand-up shapes, the sport rapidly expanded and became integrated into local culture.

Westerners got their first glimpses of surfing in 1778 when British explorer Captain James Cook sailed into Hawaii. Upon landing in the western reaches of the island chain, Cook marveled at the natives who seemed elated and entranced while riding shoreward upon the foamy crests of breaking surf. Cook and members of his crew recorded these encounters in their travel logs, and the details were later published in several European publications. Over the next 200 years, numerous other accounts of surfriding would reach the West as noted American authors such as Jack London and Mark Twain wrote detailed accounts of their observations of this strange activity. While the masses didn't start surfing themselves until much later, the civilized world could at least vicariously enjoy this amazing pastime as early as the mid-19th century.

However, by 1898, when the U.S. annexed Hawaii as a territory, surfing was on the brink of extinction. Early Christian missionaries and settlers sought to stamp out the sport because it directly conflicted with their tenets of industry and restraint of personal pleasure. Most of the Hawaiians gave up riding waves during these dark ages—with some regret, we imagine—though a few pockets of surfers still existed in isolated regions. Indeed, the ancient art may have completely disappeared if it hadn't been for one native and, ironically, one transplanted Westerner or as the Hawaiians say, "haole." At the turn of the century, a small band of people were surfing and swimming at Waikiki, and one of these riders was a haole journalist and businessman named Alexander Hume Ford. Ford was so enamored with the sport, he established a club for its preservation and promotion.

Above: *Getting paid to do something as enjoyable as riding waves makes professional surfing seem like the perfect career choice. Alex Williams slashing for dollars at Newquay, England's Rip Curl Pro.*

Right: *Costa Rica is one country that has seen an enormous economic windfall due to surf exploration. Jeremy Saukel supports the tourist industry at Pavones.*

Below: *Surfing is a largely soulful pursuit, but like all sports, competition plays an important role for many of its devotees. A young Todd Morcom cutting his competitive teeth at the ESA Championships at Cape Hatteras Lighthouse in North Carolina.*

In 1908, the Outrigger Canoe and Surfboard Club was formed, and the world's first formal surfing organization was born. Ford's group was made up of mostly haoles, so the natives formed their own surf club in 1911 called the Hui Nalu. One of the club's founders, Duke Kahanamoku, was one of the world's earliest surf explorers and would go on to become known as the father of modern surfing.

His first major accomplishments, however, occurred outside the lineup. In addition to being a top Hawaiian surfer, Duke was also a world-class swimmer. He gained global fame in 1912 during the Olympics in Sweden, where he won the gold medal in the 100-meter freestyle. Following his victory, he toured the U.S. and Europe, giving swimming demonstrations to throngs of spectators. In several key locations, Duke also hit the surf.

Visiting Ocean City, New Jersey, in 1910 for a promotional swimming tour, Kahanamoku introduced surfing to the U.S. East

Coast. Out west, another of the sport's early pioneers, a haole named George Freeth, had already surfed in California during an early exhibition at Redondo Beach in 1907, but when Duke rode his first waves in the Golden State during the '20s, people were exposed to the sport in much greater numbers due to his fame. On the international front, Duke also became one of the first worldwide surf travelers when in 1914 he was invited by Australia's New South Wales Swimming Association to visit Down Under. Kahanamoku wowed the country when he took to the surf in Freshwater Beach near Sydney, and soon, the Aussies adopted the sport into their own national lifeguarding clubs.

Above: *Dawn patrol's luring light.*
Left: *Artistic lines drawn on a watery canvas. Jason Griffith, The Abacos.*

Above: *From riding prone in the whitewater to 360 aerials, surfing's performance level is in constant evolution. Cam Anderson demonstrates a modern, fins-free style at Sebastian Inlet, Florida.*

A Cult Is Born

From the '30s through the '50s, surfing spread up and down the California coast with residents road tripping to and colonizing spots as far north as Santa Cruz. As the '60s dawned, the Southern California right-hand pointbreak known as Malibu was one of the focal points of the state's surf scene. Although surfers hate to admit it, one of the biggest explosions in American surfing was due to a short Malibu local named Kathy Kohner. Kohner hung out at the break and befriended many of the spot's male crew, learning to surf and eventually earning the nickname "Gidget." Her experiences inspired her father to write a novel titled *Gidget*, and the lighthearted tale became a best-seller. In '59, Columbia Pictures produced the movie adaptation of *Gidget*, and while the film was a little cheesy and hardly portrayed surfers in realistic light, people loved it. Soon after its

release, surfing infiltrated America's mainstream music, fashion, and language. As Drew Kampion writes in his book *Stoked: A History of Surf Culture*, "Although the surf rebels blink in the last reel when Gidget and Moondoggie return to the establishment fold after their close brush with life's leading edge, significant cultural ground was laid, on which a young generation would soon set up camp."

By the mid-'60s, larger numbers of American surfers had mapped out their country's Pacific and Atlantic coasts, searching for yet undiscovered lineups. But even earlier than that, waveriding had slowly trickled into other spots around the world. By the late '30s, surfing had been introduced to places such as Peru and Brazil in South America, as well as Durban, South Africa. Closer to home in the late '50s, U.S. surfers were exploring south of the border in Mexico and finding an entire universe of virgin waves. At the same time, parts of Europe, including France and England, also saw the introduction of modern stand-up surfriding via visiting Australians and Californians. But these first adventures were minuscule compared with the gushing torrent of worldwide surf exploration that would result from—once again—an American movie.

In 1964, California filmmaker Bruce Brown released the landmark film *The Endless Summer*, opening the floodgates to global surf exploration. The movie was a smash success all over the world, showing waveriders just what kinds of incredible adventures awaited them if they were willing to do a little globe-trotting. As Sam George said in his 2000 *Surfer Magazine* article "Sacred Hunger," "The remainder of the '60s was a magic time, the whole globe a watery Sinbad's cave full of glittering riches, an age of lost mines and treasure maps." All eyes turned to the horizon as exotic locales and world-class waves in places like Nigeria, Ghana, Senegal, New Zealand, South Africa, and Tahiti were splashed across the big screen. The climax of the film is the group's discovery of the flawless right-hander of South Africa's Cape St. Francis, which left audiences entranced. Inspired by *The Endless Summer*, surfers set out around the earth to find their own versions of the "perfect" wave.

Below: *Hawaii veteran Liam MacNamara uses the oncoming wind to glue his board to his feet as he boosts off Rocky Point's inside bowl.*

Establishment of Core Communities

About the time *The Endless Summer* debuted, Australian surfing blossomed into a thriving national sport. After Duke stopped here at the beginning of the century, surfriding in Oz was confined primarily to lifeguard organizations and surf clubs through most of the '50s, but as the '60s unfolded, it was fast becoming a pop culture phenomenon. As Nat Young writes in his book *The History of Surfing*, "What was happening in Australia was almost precisely what had happened in California earlier on. Surfing had become a cult." Surf music was taking over the airwaves, magazines like *Surfing World* were starting up, the Australian Surfriders Association was formed, and the first World Surfing Championships were held in Manly in 1964. During the late '60s and early '70s, Australians were also credited with starting the first major colonization of another one of our planet's top surf destinations—Indonesia. Because the Asian archipelago is within easy range of the Australian continent, it was only natural that the country's surfers began readily exploring Indo's myriad breaks. After only a few years, the country had developed its own thriving surf community replete with surf shops, resorts, boat services, and contests.

Such mass development was proving that surfing was indeed a powerful cultural force, and traveling waveriders were spreading it like the gospel.

During this period, another major hub within the international surfing community was developing in South Africa. As in Australia, lifeguards were the first surfriders in the country, but by the '50s, the sport had begun to flourish among all kinds of different groups. Even though waveriding began around Durban's urban line-ups, a Cape Town diver named John Whitmore is actually credited

Right: *Hawaii was, and still is, the center of the surfing universe. Mineto Ushikoshi in Backdoor.*

with pioneering many of South Africa's breaks. Whitmore explored much of the country's coastline on the west, east, and south coasts, discovering a bounty of world-class setups. With all the great waves, the number of South African surfers began multiplying rapidly, and by 1965, the South Africa Surfriders Association was established to organize all the new converts. The organization helped initiate the first major international contest into the region, Durban's Gunston 500, which would eventually become the longest-running event in the world. Modern surfing in Europe also dawned during the mid-'50s and early '60s. Up in England, local lifeguards were riding waves lying prone on wooden rescue boards as early as the '20s, but the sport really gained momentum after several Australian lifeguards visited Newquay in '62 with the latest fiberglass surfboard designs. The Aussies had their first go-out at Newquay's Great Western Beach, and as Doug Wilson and Rod Holmes say in their book *You Should Have Been Here Yesterday: The Roots of British Surfing*, "They paddled out and ripped every wave apart with a string of turns, cut backs and steep drops. This was a new game—of style and strength, power and poise." Following the Australian display of modern surfing, Cornish surfers took to the chilly North Atlantic in droves, and by the '80s, southwest England was seeing regular international contests like Cornwall's European Pro in '83 and as recently as 2001, the Rip Curl Newquay Pro in Fistral. In France, California filmmaker Peter Viertel discovered great waves along the Basque coast near Biarritz in 1956 while filming the movie adaptation of Hemingway's *The Sun Also Rises*. He and his wife got together with some locals to form the country's first surf club, and two decades after that, the French surf scene had grown to "beaucoup" proportions. In '79 the Lacanua Pro opened France to international competition, and continuing the tradition in October 2002, the Association of Surfing Professionals will hold the $300,000 Quiksilver Pro in Anglet near Biarritz.

success of the initial edition, Severson went on to make the magazine a quarterly, a bi-monthly, and finally, a monthly. Along the way, the mag's name was shortened to just *Surfer*, and it became one of the sport's most important vehicles. Following *Surfer* and then *Surfing* in the U.S., publications began popping up around the world in countries like Japan, France, Brazil, Australia, and South Africa, providing the worldwide waveriding community with the ability to see what was happening globally without leaving their couches. Leonard Lueras speaks of the magazine's impact in his book *Surfing: The Ultimate Pleasure*:

"Where else could Stinson or Ocean Beach locals learn about hydroplane board designs being wave-tested in Hawaii? Or read in-depth about last month's Bells Beach Surf Classic? Or discover that on a good day you can ride from France into Spain on a wave that curls across the mouth of the border river La Bidassoa?"

Over the years, tattered old copies of surf magazines left behind in international outposts have fallen into the hands of countless foreign groms, helping to spread the sport around the world.

Above: *Good waves aren't found only on exotic, palm tree-lined islands. City surfing in Durban, South Africa.*

Left: *South Africa's Antonio Bortoletto takes our sport to new heights in Durban.*

Pages of History

Another medium that drastically affected the expansion of our sub-culture across the world was the surf magazine. During the '60s, riding waves was seen as a spiritual pursuit, and so it made perfect sense that the genesis of the sport's bible, *Surfer Magazine*, occurred at this time. Originally a photographic supplement to John Severson's film *Surf Fever*, *The Surfer* was first published in 1960, and after the

Boom Times

By the late '70s and early '80s waveriding was becoming a big business. The establishment of professional surfing tours like the International Professional Surfers (IPS) in '76 and the Association of Surfing Professionals (ASP) in '82 made it possible for surfers to earn a living traveling the world and riding its waves. The greedy gang on Wall Street was also catching wind of this new laid-back lifestyle. The suits saw dollar signs in the white water, and as the '70s era of anti-establishment isolationism gave way to the '80s yuppie commercialism, the surf industry really started to boom. In the '80s everybody—whether they rode waves or not—wanted to look like a surfer, and companies like Quiksilver, Billabong, Gotcha, and Ocean Pacific started to manufacture the lifestyle accessories that would prove so popular.

The '80s era of big business also gave rise to the concept of commercial surf camps and private surf resorts. The famous camp at G-Land on Java developed in 1978 was one of the first of these enterprises. Housed in tree fort-like structures to keep visitors safe from man-eating tigers and venomous snakes, surfers could camp right on the reef at Grajagan, but the experience was, and still is, fairly primitive. In '82, however, two California surfers discovered a couple of world-class reefbreaks off the island of Tavarua in Fiji and soon established the first five-star surf resort. Sam George details the luxurious island in *Sacred Hunger*: "Pre-packaged perfection, the Surfer's Dream realized, but with three gourmet meals a day and a hibiscus blossom on your pillow." Tavaura quickly became known as the most extravagant surf spot on the planet, garnering the reputation as the ultimate place to visit for the sport's rich and famous. After Tavarua, a host of other such businesses have sprung up around the world with varying ranges of accommodations and amenities. There's Pico Alto Surf Camp in Peru, Playa Kandahar resort in Mexico, the Green Room Surf Camp in the Philippines, Galu Mana Surf Resort in Samoa, and Casablanca Surf Resort in Panama, to name just a few. In Indonesia alone, there are hundreds of boat charter services for surfers, ranging from the top-of-the-line technology of the *Indies Trader III* to rickety sailboats piloted by grizzled Balinese captains with no teeth. As this world of waves grows more crowded everyday, people are looking to stake out prime breaks for themselves while making a tidy profit along the way.

Above: *Getting down and dirty during a Central American surf trip.*
Right: *The advent of modern surfing forecasting units like Surfline allowed these guys to arrive at this spot in south Nicaragua right as a new swell was filling in.*

Modern Manifestations

Riding down the line into the '90s, the global surf community was united more than ever with the introduction of the Internet. Web sites like Surfline allowed state-of-the-art wave forecasting and swell prediction in every ocean on the planet, while online surf cams even provided live footage of the conditions at the best breaks. Going down to the beach and checking the surf was quickly becoming a thing of the past, and surf trips were now

being carefully planned down to the minute to coincide with the arrival of solid swell. For better or worse, much of the guesswork has been taken out of surfing, and these days knowing when and where the best waves are going to be requires nothing more than a computer and a phone line.

Even though most of the world's lineups had been charted, explored, and exploited by the '90s, there were still a handful of new destinations being discovered by an intrepid few. In 1996, the glacier-studded coast of Iceland saw its first waveriders; by 1998, India's Andaman Islands had been explored; post-cold war Russia was invaded by Californians in 2000; and in the same year, a boatload of Americans sailed and surfed the bleak, snow-covered islands and icebergs off Antarctica. That's right, Antarctica. The world's uncharted breaks have diminished significantly in the past few years, but as the Antarctic discovery shows, if you've got the resources, time, and courage to go the distance, you can still find perfect waves and have them all to yourself.

Above: *Surfers are often stereotyped by the media as lazy beach bums, but in reality, they come from all walks of life. Prominent Palm Beach, Florida, dentist Scott McCranels shatters that closed-minded way of thinking with this high-class bottom turn.*

Right: *One of the greatest things about a sport like surfing is the beauty of the playing field. Idyllic Indialantic, Florida, beachscape.*

The Spots

Wavescape provides a visual tour of some of the juicier fruits of our nomadic wanderings. Hardly an exhaustive collection, the lineups featured in this book merely scratch the surface of what's been discovered. We tried to choose a broad cross-section of global destinations that have had some historical significance or far-reaching impact on our subculture, while at the same time visiting a couple that should play prominent roles in the future. We also attempted to do all of this without exposing, and thus overcrowding, the planet's lesser-known and tighter-kept secrets. There are a few better waves than the ones mentioned in this book; however, most of these locations are well-known and widely acknowledged as some of the top spots in our global village. Any waverider seeking to learn more about this vast wilderness of surf would do well to start with the ones on these pages.

–Chris Towery, July 2002

EUROPE

With most of the recent surf media focus on exotic, tropical reefbreaks and far-off, palm tree-lined points, traveling waveriders often forget about one of the world's most consistent and incredibly varied destinations—Europe. Starting in the British Isles to the north and running down to the Portuguese shores in the south, Europe's swell-studded coastline sits like an open catcher's mitt waiting to nab any and all wave energy the Atlantic Ocean can throw its way. And because the Atlantic is the second-largest body of water on the planet, the continent gets more than its fair share of action. From Ireland's emerald green barrels and France's thumping beachbreaks to Spain's reeling rivermouths and Portugal's pummeling points, at any given moment, it's virtually guaranteed that at least one spot in Europe is firing. Add in a modern, first-world economy with a teeming waveriding population, and you've got one of the most easily accessible and surfer-friendly places on the globe.

Right: *France's beachbreaks are known by surfers worldwide for their powerful, hollow tubes. Shaun Tomson investigates this legend for himself in Biarritz.*

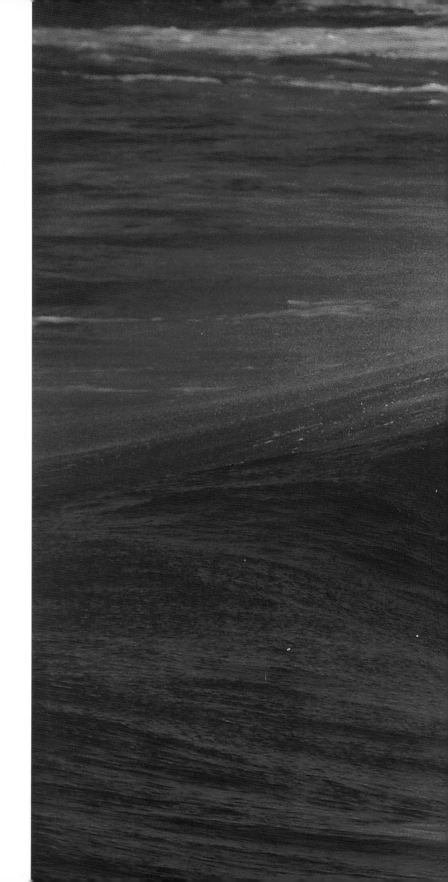

BIARRITZ, FRANCE

Back in 1956 while visiting the Basque coast of France to shoot the movie adaptation of Hemingway's *The Sun Also Rises*, filmmaker Peter Viertel discovered that the area around the town of Biarritz was loaded with hundreds of empty surf spots just waiting to be ridden. After sending for his boards in the States, Viertel pioneered several of the region's breaks and helped launch what would become one of the country's most beloved sports. Since those early days, Biarritz has grown into the epicenter of the French surf culture, and with annual pro contests and major surf businesses based here, it has also become a headquarters for the entire European waveriding community.

Once known as the Monte Carlo of Europe's west coast, Biarritz is a trendy cosmopolitan city much on the same level as South Beach, Miami. Like the American locale, Biarritz's main beach, Grande Plage, is a veritable runway of humanity: high-society types sip champagne in the outdoor cafés next to topless sunbathers while grizzled, salt-encrusted fishermen rub elbows with well-dressed businessmen. In the center of all this madness, waveriding thrives in a big way. The beach here is located inside a quarter-mile-long cove surrounded on both north and south ends by rocky headlands that

help block the onshore southwest winds. Most of the best waves are found at the southern parts of the cove with the shifting sand bottom dictating exactly where the best peaks will be at any time. Although Grande Plage is not as hard-breaking and consistent as some of the region's other waves, the surf can get very hollow on lower tides, and it's accessible to many of the downtown hotels. To the north, you'll find Anglet, which holds a bigger swell than Grande Plage. Anglet has many beachbreak peaks broken up by a series of jetties. At the north tip, just south of La Barre River, lie the peeling rights and lefts of Cavaliers, and in the south end, you'll find the rifling left-handers of the break known as V.V.F. breaking beside the town lighthouse.

Summers in Biarritz see warm, trunkable lineups crowded with hundreds of people, and during the annual invasions of the Billabong Pro surf contest in August and the Biarritz Surf Festival in July, waveriders practically take over the city. To avoid the masses at this time of year, surf early in the morning when most of the populace are sleeping or toward the evening when the sun stays up until 10 P.M. However, if you want a more laid-back atmosphere with even bigger surf, visit in the late spring and early fall when the water temps are in the 60s, and the waves fire for weeks on end with sparse crowds. But regardless of when you visit, make sure you check out the city's thriving surf industry. Quiksilver has a massive two-story surf shop right in the middle of Grande Plage, Rusty has a store here, Jeff

Hakman runs a surf school on the beaches, and Rip Curl's shop is based in town too. More and more, surfing is developing into the town's major tourist attraction, and these businesses, coupled with the big contests, stand as testament to surfing's tremendous influence on the local community. Catching those first few waves, Viertel probably never imagined that he would have such a huge impact on the culture of France.

Above: *1977 World Champion Shaun Tomson barreled in Biarritz.*

Above Left: *Grande Plage used to be a resort for Europe's elite upper crust, but more and more, this centuries old city is becoming a booming surf town.*

Far Left: *Former Australian ASP superstar Gary Elkerton liked southwest France so much, he made it his permanent home. Elkerton coming off the bottom in Grande Plage, just around the corner from his new residence in Lacanau.*

BUNDORAN, IRELAND

Positioned in the center of the North Atlantic, Ireland is one of the most surf-drenched countries in all of Europe. Every big storm system that steams across this part of the ocean sends huge tracks of swell toward the country's awaiting headlands, and even when high pressure stagnates the rest of the continent with flatness, Ireland's north-facing beaches are in prime position to score waves from storms near the Arctic. Unlike other European surf destinations, which are primarily beachbreaks, the coast of Ireland is dotted by countless reefs, points, and coves, offering a wide variety of quality setups. Of these breaks, Bundoran is considered one of the Emerald Isle's premier surf spots.

It is situated inside Donegal Bay in the northwest corner of the country, and it picks up heaps of swell from the southwest-west. The main break is known as the Peak, and it's a world-class reef located right in the middle of town at the mouth of a small river. Best at low tide, the Peak offers a long, tubing left-hander and a shorter, more punchy right with both breaking over a flat limestone reef covered with moss-like seaweed. When it's on, the left offers three emerald green barrel sections breaking for nearly 200 yards with top swell heights reaching up to ten feet. With such pristine conditions, the spot has become the focal point of the Irish surf scene, and many large contests, including the 1997 European Championships and the 2001 Quiksilver Masters, have used the reef's consistently perfect waves for their events. Unfortunately, the boom in popularity has also caused an increase in crowds, and it's not unusual to find surfers from across the globe staking out the lineup at the Peak on good swells. But crowds in Ireland are far from what they are most places. With over two-thirds of all the people living on the country's east coast and midlands, the local surfer population never reaches critical levels. Besides, even if the Peak does get crowded, take a short two-mile drive out of town, and you'll find several other great spots with probably no one out.

As you might expect, Ireland's water is quite cold. Although the Gulf Stream swings through, keeping things mostly bearable, winter water temperatures are freezing, dipping into the thirties with

Above: *It's the luck of the Irish to have such a sweet setup right in the middle of a major city. The Peak at Bundoran.*

Right: *Even though the ocean is firing on all cylinders, it's hard to take your eyes off the incredible beauty of Ireland's green, castle-studded countryside. The Peak, Bundoran.*

cold winds blasting onshore for weeks on end. Fall—between September and November—is your best bet, as the large systems start pumping in regular swells and you can get away with 4/3s and booties. But regardless of the chill in the lineup, you'll discover that the Irish are some of the warmest, most friendly people on Earth. One of the best parts of the Ireland experience is found in the local pubs, where almost the entire population goes to socialize. There's nothing quite like relaxing and socializing in an authentic Irish pub after a smoking session at the Peak. And don't forget to check out the countryside, too. The landscape is littered with rolling green hills, deep lakes, and centuries-old castles. Between Ireland's great surf, the stunning beauty of the land, and the down-home hospitality of its locals, you'll totally forget that you're surfing in a place closer to the Arctic Circle than the equator.

COXOS, PORTUGAL

One of the greatest advantages to surfing in Portugal is that loads of world-class waves lie within easy reach of the Lisbon capital and its international airport. Just a few hours' drive north of this metropolis, you'll find hundreds of points, reefs, and beaches with consistent surf almost year-round. You could easily spend your entire trip just in this area and never want for lack of surf. And if you're into challenging, hard-breaking waves, you'll most likely head toward the town of Ericeira, where the pummeling reefbreak known as Coxos waits to test your mettle.

Coxos is a right point/reefbreak setup located on the north end of a small bay, in front of a perilously shallow rock outcropping. The spot is legendary among Portuguese and other European surfers for its board-breaking power. Here, waves come out of very deep water and hurl themselves over the bay's rocky shallows, forming long, grinding right-hand barrels. Boasting sharp rocks and heavy currents, just paddling out at Coxos can be dangerous, so this is one spot better left to the more experienced when it gets big. Paddle out in the middle of the bay where there is usually a comfortable channel and head toward the main peak. At the peak, the wave jacks up and offers intense drops followed by a 100-yard-long roping wall. The best surf comes from the north-northwest, which is the most common swell direction during the winter, so expect super-consistent waves up to 15 feet during this time of year. The ideal tide is between low and mid-tide when the water is shallow enough to make the wave steep, but just deep enough to cushion its bone-crunching force.

Crowds double the danger factor on some days as the small takeoff zone becomes packed with throngs of surfers and bodyboarders from the outlying areas. However, as with most heavy-water breaks, the masses tend to thin when things get really serious. Outside of the crowds, there are a few other hazards. You'll need to bring a fullsuit for the cold water and

booties for the sharp rocks and urchins and, if you like to party, bring along plenty of aspirin too. Ericeira is a lot smaller than Lisbon and lies dormant most of the week, but on weekends and holidays, the town comes alive with hundreds of people looking to celebrate. Locals like the nightlife, and with good food, great wine, and intoxicating spirits like absinthe available for cheap prices, things can get out of hand very easily. Exercise moderation with the nightlife because after all, the most intense action and cheapest thrills in Ericeira can be found just offshore in Coxos' thumping rights.

Above: *The area around Portugal's capital city of Lisbon is loaded with hundreds of world-class spots just like this. Reeling rights off Coxos.*

Right: *Coxos breaks over a perilously shallow rock reef, but with perfect pits like this, surfers have no problem risking life and limb.*

EL QUEMAO, LANZAROTE

Bearing the full force of North Atlantic winter storms, Spain's Canary Islands off Africa are known as the "Hawaii of the Atlantic," and the spot known as El Quemao could easily rank as the chain's Pipeline. Located on the island of Lanzarote—one of the most surf-laden destinations in the world—El Quemao is a pummeling left-hander that breaks over a dangerous, lava-encrusted reef. It's definitely one of the most powerful spots in the Canaries, and a high level of respect and caution coupled with many years of heavy-water experience are required before one should even think about surfing here.

The name El Quemao translates to "The Burn" in English, and this moniker is an apt title for such a punishing break. With no continental shelf to speak of, massive groundswells out of the west and northwest strike Lanzarote's volcanic reefs with all their bone-crushing power still intact. The resulting leviathans throw out massive A-frames over a perilously shallow bottom, which has inflicted more than a few major injuries. Although the right is surfed occasionally, the real focus is on the left. Breaking best in the winter from six to 15 feet, El Quemao's left-hander has two sections—a main peak and an inside bowl. The outside peak is a little less steep than the inside, but it's still pretty hairy. Each zone offers heaving barrels, but farther toward shore, the pits can close out in some very nasty ways. As the wave reaches the end section, it can either shut down in a skull-crushing closeout or propel you through its bowels via a frothy foamball to the shoulder. The object of the place—and the best way to avoid the first option—is to consistently find the outside peaks that line up across the entire two sections and fade them through the inside bowl.

This world-class setup is situated directly in front of a boulder-studded harbor wall in the quaint little village of La Santa on the island's northwest coast. This wall houses the local peanut gallery on the epic days as people gather here to watch surfers test their mettle against El Quemao and offer their vocal commentary on each ride. The spot generally tends to be one of the least-crowded waves in the area—probably due to its black diamond rating—so if you venture out, you'll probably share the place with only a few other big guns. Bring a big-wave board, full wetsuit in the winter, springsuit at other times, and booties all year for the sharp bottom and sea urchins. And if you're going to charge "The Burn" on the biggest days, helmets are an excellent idea, too.

Above: *This shot of El Quemao may not look that dangerous, but check out the jagged lava in the foreground. That's exactly what lies only a few feet beneath the surface out in the lineup.*

Right: *Heading out to feel "The Burn" at El Quemao, Lanzarote.*

FISTRAL, ENGLAND

Although most people probably wouldn't consider England a prime surfing destination, the country not only boasts great waves on all of its coastlines, but also harbors one of Europe's largest populations of surfers. The southwest region of Cornwall is the country's busiest waveriding area, and here you'll find a large number of local riders as well as tons of surf-related businesses. The beachbreaks along this stretch of coast have even hosted several international professional surfing competitions such as the 2001 Rip Curl Newquay Pro, and with that kind of attention, it's no wonder that Newquay is known as England's waveriding capital.

The U-shaped cove of Fistral is Newquay's most popular surfing beach, and it's divided into three major breaks. The south end is known as South Fistral, and is primarily a high-tide left-hander, which breaks next to the southernmost headland. The middle peak— North Fistral—is an A-frame offering both rights and lefts, which favor low to mid tides. And finally, the northernmost break—Little Fistral— is another split peak, which is found inside the north headland, breaking over slabs of sand-covered rock reef and offering thumping barrels on the lower tides. All three peaks are pretty mellow, possessing mostly forgiving bottoms and fairly easy-breaking lineups. But even though Fistral offers no really heavy surf, it's very consistent, partially blocked from the persistently onshore southwest winds, and breaks through most every tide.

Located directly in the teeth of the North Atlantic storm track, there's plenty of surf in the area, but Ireland shadows Cornwall, preventing it from receiving all but the biggest northwesterly swells. The majority of wave action coming to this region is from the southwest-west, and swell heights can reach up to twelve feet on the biggest days.

Fistral, as well as Newquay's other beaches, can get extremely crowded with surfers and tourists during summer. From June through September, people from across the country descend upon Newquay for holidays, and because this is also the region's high season for flatspells, it can be an extremely frustrating time of year for waveriders. Surfers are better off coming during the fall and winter months when the Atlantic churns up classic groundswells with nearly deserted beaches. However, the trade off for less crowds is much colder water. But with the Gulf Stream nearby, this is one of England's mildest zones, and although a fullsuit is a year-round necessity, hoods and gloves are needed only from December through March. So if you're looking for a good place to start a European surf trip, Fistral's mild climate, easy waves, and well-entrenched surf culture is a welcoming gateway to the rest of this swell-saturated continent.

Above: *Adrian Buchan doing the shoebreak shuffle at Fistral during the Rip Curl Board Masters.*

Right: *Newquay is the starting point for many international surfing trips. Australia's Kirk Flintoff kicks off his vacation with this north Fistral slash.*

Left: *Peeling A-frames like this are the main reason the ASP chose Fistral Beach as one of its top European contest sites.*

HOSSEGOR, FRANCE

The French surf scene is one of the world's wildest. Ever since surfing became popular here in the late '70s and early '80s, the country's southwest coast has become a mecca for Europe's waveriding crowd. Legions of travelers descend every summer and fall to ride some of the world's finest beachbreaks amid an intense, party-till-dawn nightlife. You'll find an abundance of surf shops, warm lineups with thumping barrels, and carnival-like surf contests such as the annual Rip Curl Pro popping up during these months. Add in some of the world's best wine and food, and a very relaxed culture, and you've got a destination like no other.

Although there are great breaks up and down France's southwest coast, one of the major hubs for surfers and some of the best waves can be found in the town of Hossegor. There's a deep-sea trench just offshore that funnels large swells directly into this six-mile-long stretch of beach. Unimpeded by shallow water, these waves unload monstrous, sand-spitting barrels just yards from the shoreline. The intensity and power of Hossegor's surf is often compared to Mexico's Puerto Escondido, with wave heights reaching up to 15 feet, so it's a good idea to bring boards with a little extra

Above: *Hossegor's barrels break so close to the beach that you can get drenched by the spit just by standing on the sand.*

length—up to a semi-gun—for the bigger days. Almost all of the spots near Hossegor are beachbreaks, and several peaks dot the coast from L'Epi Nord at the south end to La Graviere in the central zone, and Les Estagnots in the north. Tidal changes in France can range up to 14 feet, so finding the best waves among these different lineups is heavily dependent on being dialed into the local tide charts and lucking into those moments when the sandbanks are just right. If you go in the summer, the water is trunkable, but during spring and fall you'll need anything from a warm springsuit to a fullsuit. Winter is cold and often stormy, requiring 4/3s with booties.

If you find yourself in Hossegor during the warm months, you'll quickly realize that the sun and surf aren't the only things that get hot. Hossegor's nightlife can really heat up, so practice moderation if you plan on making it out for the dawn patrol. But even if you find yourself tired and out of sorts, stumbling over the wide dune line at noon, there's no better way to clear your head than by getting spit out of a few dredging pits in Hossegor's heaving hollows.

Above: *A deep-water trench just offshore Hossegor allows the Atlantic to unload on the city's beaches with all of its open-ocean power still intact. Simon Law runs for cover in southwest France.*

Below: *Tahiti's Vetea David learns that Hossegor's beachbreaks can barrel just as hard as some of his favorite reefs back home.*

MUNDAKA, SPAIN

In the Basque region near the northeast corner of Spain lies one of Europe's finest lefts—Mundaka. This legendary lineup is located in the Guernika rivermouth next to the little fishing village for which the break is named. It's a fickle spot and may take a while to get good, but when just the right elements of northwest swell, low tide, and perfectly shaped sand finally come together, the spot offers a world-class left-hand tube reeling for over 200 yards and rivaling any rivermouth on the planet.

Mundaka is Spain's most well-known spot and has become an extremely popular destination for surfers from all over the world. The Association of Surfing Professionals holds regular pro events here like the $250,000 Billabong Pro, and with that much money on the line, you know the place must be something special. During the fall and winter months, when swells swing in from the northwest, they hit the triangle-shaped sandbank at the mouth of the Guernika and jack up into steep barreling peaks. If you survive the insane drop at the top of the point, the challenge has just begun. Immediately after making it off the bottom, a gaping tube chases you at breakneck speeds for hundreds of yards, an experience similar in adrenaline-pumping excitement to the running of the bulls in nearby Pamplona. On this run, however, you'll be chased by grinding barrels with thick lips, rather than furious bovines with sharp horns. Once the race is on, this beast of a wave reels relentlessly down the point, and the top-to-bottom pits just don't stop. As you speed down the line, scoring several shacks on one wave is a very real possibility, and if you catch it on one of the biggest days, when it can reach 15 feet, you'll need a real knowledge of tube-riding and a reliable gun to avoid being gored by Mundaka's punishing lips.

But on the more mellow side, the break does offer a relatively painless paddle-out. Simply jump in the water at the harbor

Above: *Symmetrical lines of swell unloading next to Mundaka's famous church.*
Right: *Even when it's small, Mundaka's barrels can be legendary.*

near the famous castle-like church on the point, and let the fast-flowing river pull you out into the lineup. From there, you'll take your place in the take-off zone with the locals and visiting waveriders: crowds range from moderate to heavy, depending on the swell and tide. And once you manage to snag a good one through to the inside, avoid the exhausting paddle back by riding the white water into the sandy beach and heading once again for the harbor jump-off. Fullsuits are necessary year-round because of a cold offshore current, and when it gets really big, helmets are a good idea, too, because like the Pamplona run, sometimes people forget that those horns are for real.

SUPERTUBOS, PORTUGAL

As the westernmost country in Europe, Portugal's coastline acts as a wave magnet for surf thrown up by the Atlantic's powerful storms. From late fall to early spring—November through April—huge frontal systems sweep across the open ocean, bombarding its shores with some of the continent's most consistent surf. Smack in the middle of this swell-inundated coastline lies one of Portugal's most famous and hardest-breaking spots—Supertubos.

The name alone should give you some idea of the place's quality. Located just south of the fishing town of Peniche, Supertubos offers some of Europe's best beachbreak barrels, and just about every magazine article or book on Portugal surfing will feature at least one photo of somebody slotted in Super's gaping pits. As a sand-bottomed beachbreak, these tubes break in several shifting peaks that form into prime, A-frame setups, up and down the shoreline. The wave is extremely fast wall with ruler-edged tubes going both ways, but the lefts seem to offer the best rides with longer shoulders and fewer closeouts. The spot's swell window stretches wide from northwest to southwest, and although the norths are more consistent, it's often the more southerly angles that offer the most pristine conditions. Supertubos is also one of the places to head for when the country gets a large swell, as it will break up to 12 feet. But be warned: even though the bottom is covered with sand, these larger waves explode with awesome ferocity over dangerously shallow bars.

Supertubos is easy to find—just follow the smell of rotting fish. A cannery sits only a short distance from the lineup, and when the offshores blow hard enough, the stench out in the water can become overpowering. But be thankful for the odor, because the offshores are the main reason the beach isn't one huge closeout. Outside of stinky fish, there is also some crowding. With such a great setup, surfers from across the country and around the planet fill the lineup when the waves are good. If this happens, things can get a bit tense, but most of the surfers here are fairly good-tempered and friendly, not bothering those who show some respect and manners. The weather in this region is well-tempered as well, with temperatures never getting too hot or too cold. Part of this is due to a chilly ocean upwelling offshore. Because of these cold currents, the Atlantic in this region never really rises much above 60 degrees, and these temperatures tend to regulate the weather on land, making it quite pleasant year-round. However, because of the cool water, a fullsuit is needed almost all year, except in the dog days of summer when the brisk salt water will provide a welcome relief from the hot sun. The cold water, crowds, and stench all might make the place seem less appealing, but after a few perfect pits at Supertubos, you'll barely remember any of the spot's maladies.

Above: *The beach at Supertubos, Portugal.*
Right: *An authentic bird's-eye view of Portugal's Supertubos, which lives up to its namesake.*

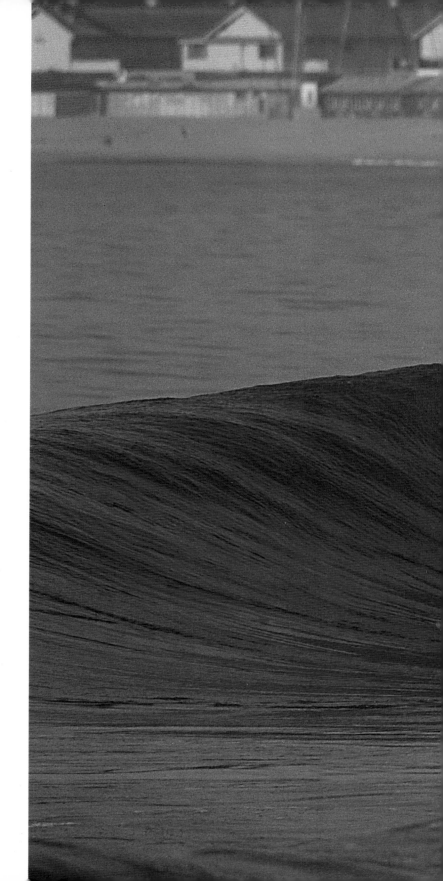

AFRICA

While mainstream society has long viewed Africa as
a continent with a bounty of wild animals and nature
preserves, surfers have seen this mysterious land in
a different light. Ever since the peeling rights off
South Africa's Cape St. Francis were splashed
across movie screens in Bruce Brown's *The Endless
Summer*, surfers have been drawn to the continent
for its limitless surf potential. And over the past four
decades, waveriding explorers have discovered and
tamed a bounty of spots. From the legendary freight-
train rights at Jeffrey's Bay and the pounding urban
lineups around Durban to the exotic desert points in
central Morocco, Africa has become one of the
planet's ultimate waveriding experiences. It has
evolved into a destination all serious surf travelers
must visit at least once in their lives.

Right: *Just to the north of New Pier, the Bay of Plenty used to be
Durban's main surf venue. Although recent beach
construction greatly diminished the spot's quality, on good
days it still offers pristine, cylindrical right-handers.*

ANCHOR POINT, MOROCCO

As a popular stop on the European hippie trail in the '60s, Morocco in northwest Africa saw hordes of international travelers as early as four decades ago. And because surfing was so closely tied to the counterculture movement of that era, many of these longhaired, bell-bottomed visitors came home with wild tales of perfect, empty waves breaking all winter long in a relatively mild climate. Since those early explorations, Morocco's coast has become a wintertime haven for European waveriders who descend every year to ride the country's super-consistent breaks in one of the world's most exotic cultural settings. Morocco boasts waves all along its largely northwest-facing coastline, from Casablanca's consistent beachbreaks in the north to the empty lineups bordering the Sahara Desert in the south. However, the centrally located right-hander known as Anchor Point is probably the most famous break in the country.

Located about an hour and a half north of the town of Agadir, Anchor Point is named for an old anchor-making factory whose ruins are still visible near the break today. The spot is one of many long, right pointbreaks located in this region, but Anchors is popular for being one of the more sheltered spots and also because it holds some of the biggest swells. The wave breaks inside a long bend in the rocky headland, and on the larger days, the surf can peel all the way into the next town of Tarhazoute over a half mile away. Because it's more sheltered than some of the other spots up-coast, Anchor Point needs a larger northwest swell—about six feet—to really start working. But during winter, from December through March, the place fires almost weekly. To reach the take-off spot, surfers should walk out as far as possible on a natural rock jetty at the top of the point and jump off into the water, timing the sets carefully to avoid a fearsome pummeling on the paddle-out. Once outside, the wave is a long, walled-up right-hander breaking from 15 to 18 feet. Although it doesn't break with top-to-bottom force in its entirety, barrel sections frequently pop up on the ideal lower tides, and waves can be ridden over 500 yards. As mentioned before, Anchor Point is popular, so when it's good, expect to share the rights with medium- to large-sized crowds of mostly locals. Also, because the

best swells hit during the winter, you'll need a fullsuit for the cold water, and with urchins infesting the inside rocks, booties are a good idea too.

In addition to the excellent surf, the Moroccan culture is one of the most exotic in all the world, featuring a veritable cornucopia of otherworldly sights, sounds, and smells. Probably the best example of this amazing scene is inside the huge, open-air markets known as "souks" in cities like Agadir and Marrakesh. Make sure you include at least one stop to these incredible bazaars on your surf trip. But keep in mind that this is a largely Muslim country with strict cultural mores and attitudes. Alcohol is almost totally prohibited, women should avoid wearing revealing clothes, and touching food or another person with your left hand is taboo. In the wake of September 11, be especially careful not to disrespect the culture, and pay close attention to travel advisories before planning your trip. But if you maintain an attitude of respect and are sensible with your behavior, you'll uncover a mysterious, yet beautiful people and a treasure trove of unbelievable surf.

Far left: *The African sun setting over Anchor Point.*

Left: *Rustic accommodation along Morocco's central coast.*

Above: *Local ripper banking off the top of Anchor's mid-break.*

CAVE ROCK, SOUTH AFRICA

Hosting the largest population of surfers in the country, Durban—appropriately nicknamed "Surf City"—has so many user-friendly peaks, it often spawns packed lineups. But a 15-minute drive around the Bluff Peninsula reveals a wave that is sure to deter the fainthearted—the thumping right-hander known as Cave Rock. The Brighton Beach swimming pool and a giant rock on the beach marks the spot. While other breaks in the subtropical Kwazulu Natal region are generally safer and more manageable, "The Rock" is one of the heaviest—and during optimal conditions one of the most prized—tube-riding waves in all of South Africa.

On bigger swells, Cave Rock is the focal point of Durban surfing. Like Oahu's Backdoor Pipeline or Off The Wall, this vicious wave is a challenge for surfers of all mettle. Its ledgy cylinders result from southerly swells coming out of deep water and striking a flat but deadly rock shelf dusted with sand. Needless to say, the experienced Durban tubedwellers reign supreme here. The 1977 International Professional Surfers World Champion Shaun Tomson cut his teeth in the perilously shallow pits, and through the years, South African lensman Chris Van Lennep has helped elevate the spot's status to nothing short of legendary with his stellar water photography. Tidal changes greatly affect the conditions at Cave Rock, which often borders on rippable and barely rideable—peaking up like an inviting beachbreak one day and rifling like a challenging point the next. It's a somewhat fickle wave, but when it's on, The Rock is always thick and dredging. It works best on either a cyclone swell coming off Madagascar or a long-interval, southwest groundswell—six foot or bigger—and helped by a low to incoming tide. On dead-low tides, any takers should exercise caution. With only a few feet of water between rider and reef, this place can break you. Offshores are a rarity in this part of the country, but surfers do find Cave Rock blessed with blue-green glassiness when cold fronts pass over the continental landmass during the Southern Hemisphere winter. This occurs mostly in the mornings, too.

Like most dumpy reefbreaks, Cave Rock's best view can be seen only when rushing it deep under the lip and behind the peak.

Above: *South African pro Frankie Oberholzer steers a careful line through Cave Rock's frighteningly square tube section.*

Tubes right off the drop are a common occurrence. While the take-off zone might not be quite as concentrated as some Hawaiian bully-breaks, this place requires the same type of attitude when dealing with the power. Commitment and respect are important. The same goes with the locals. Cave Rock regulars are extremely tuned in to its swaying moods, live by their spot, and don't take kindly to shoulder hoppers or loudmouths—so do yourself a favor and tread softly. One should also think "Hawaii" when choosing equipment. Speed is key. Full wetsuits are needed only on the coldest mornings of the winter. Apart from the deadly rips and bone-crushing slabs of water, the great white menace at Cave Rock is comparatively minor next to other South African surfbreaks, as most Durban beaches are equipped with shark nets. Given the many other hazardous attributes, though, when Cave Rock is doing its thing, it is a no-nonsense wave for experts only.

Below, inset: *One should savor every opportunity to drive a good bottom turn at Cave Rock. After all, the wave is a barrel off the bat most of the time.*

Below: *You have to ask yourself before you paddle out, "Is this tube worth risking a concussion?" You bet it is.*

JEFFREY'S BAY, SOUTH AFRICA

South Africa's Jeffrey's Bay has long been called the planet's best right. It's even been described as the finest wave in all the world. Regardless of what you label it, J-Bay is inarguably one of the Earth's most epic surf spots, and if you're looking for a place that'll show you just what the world's oceans are capable of producing in terms of all-time waves, then Jeffrey's Bay is definitely one location you must visit.

Located west of Port Elizabeth in the central region of South Africa's swell-studded coastline, J-Bay is a right-hand pointbreak like no other. During the Southern Hemisphere's winter, which runs from June through August, huge storms spinning out of the Roaring Forties track up toward the Cape of Good Hope and push massive southwest groundswells toward Jeffrey's waiting lava reef point. Luckily, this heavy load of surf also coincides with the year's most plentiful offshores, called "Land Breezes" by locals.

Like most pointbreaks of any real size, J-Bay is divided into several sections rather than one long, symmetrical swell line. But unlike other points, Jeffrey's holds a bounty of five distinct zones: Magnatubos, Boneyards, Supertubos, Impossibles, and The Point. Starting at Magnatubos, which is the farthest up the point, you'll find a sectiony right that peaks up but rarely lines up all the way through. After that, comes Boneyards, a hollow walled-up section that breaks better than Magnas but tends to close out upon reaching the next and most popular zone, Supertubos. Supers is aptly named, as it's an unbelievably fast and walled-up wave, which pitches out big, throaty barrels. If you've outrun Supers' speedy walls and exploding lip line, then you arrive at Impossibles. This section is so named for the fact that it almost always contains sections that close down at one point or another, making it nearly "impossible" to ride all the way through its 150-yard raceway. If you do accomplish the impossible, however, you'll find yourself at the final section known as The Point. Usually more forgiving than the other parts, this slower section will give your legs and lungs a rest from the intense workout you've endured to make it this far, and as you reach the final closeout at the end of The Point, you'll be thankful that's all J-Bay has to offer.

Above: *Timing the sets for the paddle out on J-Bay's lava rock point.*

But making it around all the different sections isn't the only thing you have to be concerned with at J-Bay. First you need the right equipment. For the cold water and jagged rocks, bring at least a 3/2 mm fullsuit and booties. Then you'll need a board that can handle the breaks' speed and size. When it's small, a racy shortboard with a little extra length is okay, but over six feet and it's time to break out a gunnier board. A group of locals known as the "White Shirts" will let you know if you're taking too many waves or getting out of line with your attitude. But much more hazardous than the White Shirts are the white sharks. These predators are abundant in Indian Ocean waters, and in 1998 alone, there was a record number of 18 shark attacks in the Eastern Cape region of South Africa, which houses J-Bay. Most everyone agrees that Jeffrey's Bay is one of the world's most treasured surfing locales, and the sharks may just be nature's way of letting us know that her riches always come at a price.

Left, inset: *Many surfers would kill to have a backyard view like this one.*

Above: *High speed carve along the tube's inside racetrack.*

NEW PIER, SOUTH AFRICA

Boasting the largest population of surfers and surf-related businesses in the country, the town of Durban is the waveriding capital of South Africa. The area's beaches are located near the bustling center of the city with easy access to over 12 different spots, ranging from mellow, forgiving beachbreaks to explosive, barreling reefs. For years, these urban lineups have hosted major professional surfing contests, such as the Gunston 500 and the Mr. Price Pro, which helped produce a world champion professional surfer like local Shaun Tomson. With such big events and great surfers, along with the regular visits from many other international travelers, Durban has planted deep surfing roots in South Africa's culture.

A string of piers and groins along the city's central beaches have long been the center of Durban's numerous breaks. However, the remodeling of several of these structures years ago has negatively affected some of the lineups while making others much better. Consequently, the Bay of Plenty, which used to be the main break, is now a shadow of its former magnificence, while just to the south, New Pier has stepped up as the leading spot. New Pier is found at the southern end of Dairy Beach, and the wave is a barreling right-hander that breaks down the north end of the structure. Peaking up just outside the pier's tip, the waves can peel for over 150 yards while throwing out spitting tubes from take-off to kick-out. The spot works best at low tide with offshore southwest winds grooming the watery faces into kegging pits. Some of the best swells come during the Southern Hemisphere's summer from November through April when cyclones near Madagascar send in booming easterly groundswells. However, these storms are infrequent, so for more consistency, try winter from May to October for frequent southerly swells from the Roaring Forties. The largest surf during any given time will run up to 12 feet, but most of these lineups seem to handle smaller, six- to eight-feet waves, better.

Durban is situated inside a subtropical climate zone with very mild temperatures for nearly the entire year. So if you come in

Above: *You can see from this shot of a deeply pitted Simon Nicholson why many locals call New Pier the best wave in all of Durban.*

Right: *The construction of New Pier not only provided a fantastic place to smack the lip, like Dane Patterson demonstrates here, but it also established a convenient, front-row perch for area photographers to catch the action.*

winter, bring a fullsuit only for the height of the season, and the rest of the year, you can get away with a springsuit or boardshorts. Although this stretch of South African coast is infamous for harboring large man-eating Great White sharks, almost all the town's beaches are protected by offshore nets that prevent the fish from getting near the swimming and surfing areas. However, if you venture outside the nets, keep a keen eye out for any potential predators lurking below—spots just outside the city have some of the highest rates of attacks in the world. But the great thing about Durban is that you needn't go far to find great waves because just about all of the region's top spots, like New Pier, are just steps from the center of town.

ST. LEU, REUNION ISLAND

Reunion Island, a territory of France lying east of Madagascar, is one of the most sensuous locales in the world. With a luscious tropical climate, several scenic volcanoes dotting the interior, both black and white sand beaches skirting the coasts, and consistent surf breaking along perfectly sculpted coral reefs, it's no wonder the Association of Surfing Professionals chose the island—its premier left-hander St. Leu in particular—as one of the world tour's prime stops in the '90s.

Located just outside a sparkling lagoon, St. Leu seems like it was designed with surfers in mind. Depending on the swell direction, the wave typically begins with an easy-access take-off followed by a ridiculously roping wall, allowing for a series of experimental carves and long section floaters. As it bends down the line into shallower water, the wave increases—sometimes doubles—in height before hitting the second bowl where the bottom drops out, offering a meaty barrel section. Southwest swells powered by the Roaring Forties off South Africa work best at St. Leu, and these can occur any time throughout the year but are less common during the Southern Hemisphere summer. A general rule of thumb is the more west the swell is, the throatier the barrel. The more south it is, the more smackable the wall—especially for backsiders. The wave generally works from three feet up, but typically closes out after ten feet.

St. Leu is one of the most notorious shark-infested areas in the world, and attacks on surfers are fairly common. Despite the abundance of corduroy sets on better days, crowds can get quite dense and territorial disputes often turn violent. Other nuisances include urchins and fire coral, both of which are difficult to avoid at lower tides. Wetsuits are hardly necessary, although a thin springsuit might help cut down on chills from morning breezes—not to mention reef abrasions.

St. Leu is the kind of wave some surfers fall into a mystical, somewhat obsessive relationship with. Just ask former Pipeline Master Rob Machado, who lists it as one of his favorite waves. Lucky for Rob, he married Reunion native Patou Locame in 1998, thus becoming a lifetime local. And who can blame him? After all this is the kind of wave you daydreamed about while doodling in your school books.

Above: *Another left bends along Reunion Island's reef under the watchful eyes of several spectators.*

Right: *With its endlessly folding pocket, St. Leu might be the best wave in the world for backhand surfing.*

Asia

Nowhere on Earth so singularly defines island
perfection as Asia, the land of the flawless reefbreak.
Indonesia and The Philippines—the waves in this
region continue to represent the finest in waveriding
stoke, existing among the most exotic and
spellbinding cultures outside of the Western world.
Graced with seemingly unending swell from such
glorious wavemakers like the Roaring Forties, the
reefs of Asia take on a heavenly appearance when
wind and tide cooperate in the least. And the tropical
landscapes housing the dreamy waves make these
spots unmissable on the serious surf traveler's
itinerary. Whether you're burning through the g-
forces at Uluwatu or stretching out in the beautiful
bowls of Nias, prepare to have your mind blown
sooner or later on some Asian reef. Here the waves
are hollow, symmetrical, and—more often than not—
as fast as they come.

Right: *Surfing in the Indonesian archipelago can really be
summed up in three words—exhilarating, treacherous,
beautiful. Nias is but one wave representing all of
these qualities.*

CLOUD NINE, SIARGAO ISLAND, PHILIPPINES

Introduced to the world in 1992 by *Surfer Magazine* photographer John Callahan, along with professional surfers Evan Slater and Taylor Knox, the Philippine dream known as Cloud Nine is a keynote in the song of discovery. Located in the town of General Luna on Siargao Island's east coast, the spot received its title from Callahan, who had a sweet tooth for the tasty Philippine candy bars of the same name. Cloud Nine is located just inside the 10,000-meter-deep Philippine Trench; thus the energy strikes the shallow reefs of Siargao unhindered. Although the break can be quite fickle depending on how much typhoon activity is present, when it's good—like six feet, glassy, and sucking dry—it can remain so all day, every day, for weeks. Put simply, every wave at Cloud Nine is a tube. Seeming to rise up out of nowhere, the wave throws out a split peak with a shorter but still hollow left. The right, though, is what keeps people coming back for more. The wave sucks water off the bottom, almost appearing as a closeout; however, once the rider is inside the pocket, it hits a bend in the reef and shoulders off into the most perfect barrel imaginable. Rideable at mid to high tide, Cloud Nine is easy enough to set up, as most waves do the same thing. It cannot be charged anywhere but from the pit, though. The extreme bowliness will quickly pitch any shoulder hoppers. This wave only allows a surfer to push himself deeper and deeper until he's confidently backdooring the slots. However, getting too deep will warrant a violent confrontation with the reef.

With the water as warm as anywhere in the world, no wetsuit is necessary here, but a rashguard or T-shirt might be a good idea to aid in protection from the brutal ultraviolet rays overhead. Access to this break is easy, as there is now a wooden walkway that winds over the bothersome crevices in the reef. One should bring several backup boards to Cloud Nine, as this wave is bound to snap one or two per quiver. Pintails with lots of rocker are key. And a little extra length can't hurt. Remember, this wave is for tube-riding—not chop-hopping.

Cloud Nine picks up swells generated in the western Pacific by typhoons running the track from Guam to Luzon, most typically from September to December. Conveniently, this is also the time when offshore winds associated with monsoons are more likely. Since Cloud Nine's discovery, more resorts and restaurants have popped up in General Luna and the town even hosts a local surf contest and festival called the Siargao Cup. The fresh influx of touring surfers gives local people more money-making opportunities than ever, and many are exposed to new things they never knew existed—like surfing. Just as with many underdeveloped coastal societies, local surfers at Cloud Nine are extremely in touch with the lineup, and some of their tube-riding abilities are uncanny. But despite the new attention on the absurdly perfect wave at Cloud Nine, there are thousands of surf spots in the Philippines waiting to be explored. Add to that all the better-known points, reefs, and beaches waiting short rides away from General Luna, and you have a wave-rich region with unlimited potential.

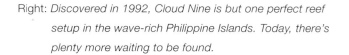

Right: *Discovered in 1992, Cloud Nine is but one perfect reef setup in the wave-rich Philippine Islands. Today, there's plenty more waiting to be found.*

DESERT POINT, LOMBOK, INDONESIA

A surf spot doesn't have to be consistent to be world-class, even in the swell-saturated Indonesian archipelago. A perfect left in a land of perfect lefts, Desert Point, also called Bangko-Bangko by the locals, is located on the island of Lombok, directly east of Bali. It's been referred to by some seasoned Indonesian frequenters as the best wave in the world—more manageable than G-Land, longer than Padang Padang, and more hollow than Uluwatu.

Desert Point is also one of the most fickle waves in the world, rideable on a decent swell and at low tides only. When checking this break at high tide, even on a good swell, one might find nothing but a one-foot wave lapping along the point, barely rideable and certainly not worth wasting a day at. But when the tide drops, this otherwise frail wave can quickly turn into a five- or six-foot dream point. When it's working, Desert starts with an easy take-off. This is where the wave is its smallest, but as it rifles along the point, it increases—sometimes doubles—in height, offering several thick barrel sections. In between tubes, Desert backs off ever so slightly to let the rider get a few turns in, making it the quintessential reef-point. Barrel-cutback-barrel-floater-barrel . . . you get the picture. This wave turns on in the blink of an eye, and it turns off just as quickly. It is best during the Southern Hemisphere winter, when swells are more predominant. The southeast trades greatly help this wave take shape. Because of its fickle but magical reputation, not to mention the large number of boat charters running out of Bali, the lineup at Desert Point can get quite aggressive. And surfers who don't follow the regular drop-in rules can put other surfers in the water in serious jeopardy, as Desert's reef is deceptively shallow.

Another hazard worth mentioning is the deadly current running out to sea via the Lombok Strait. When tides drop, this current sucks out with jaw-dropping speed, and surfers have been known to get sucked all the way around the point. Remember, there's nothing between you and Antarctica here, so if you're going in the current, you're probably already gone. Be careful and pay attention to what's happening in the lineup.

A session at Desert Point can go down a variety of ways. You might catch nothing at all if the proper elements fail to come together. You might catch it going off, and with only sixty people in the lineup to share the perfection with. Or you might catch it empty, glassy, and flawless. Then you can raise your fists to the sky and scream with elation. After all, this is the kind of wave that makes you proud you surfed and proud you caught it good. It's Desert Point. When you score, it's one of the best bragging rights there is.

Right: *Fickle and rideable at low tide only, the waves at Lombok's Desert Point might be the best in a land of perfect lefts. A rare one goes by untouched.*

G-LAND, JAVA, INDONESIA

Perhaps the world's longest, most perfect left-hander, the phenomenon known as G-Land lies off the eastern side of Grajagan Bay on the southwest corner of Java. The first surf camp was started there in the late '70s by Mike Boyum, and since then several other camps have popped up, mostly operated by Balinese businessmen. Part of the Plengkung National Forest, G-Land is, quite literally, right on the edge of a jungle. A generator powers all the electricity to the camps, and it shuts down at 10:30 P.M. every night, leaving a surfer alone with his thoughts and the eerie sounds of the jungle.

The waves at G-Land break over a wide and expansive coral reef curving into the bay. Southerly swells from the Indian Ocean make the many sections come to life in different ways. The first section of the G-Land setup is Kong's. Kong's breaks in deep water and is one of the best options on smaller swells. It's a long walk over the reefs to get there, but this spot offers plenty of rippable sections and even tubes on bigger swells. But if the waves really start to turn on, a better bet than Kong's is Moneytrees. This section is G-Land's mid-break, capable of holding swells up to ten feet and bigger and providing the archetypal G-Land wave—long, shapely, and barreling off its face. The take-off point can be difficult to find, and the reef can get super-shallow at lower tides, but a good ride here will set the tempo for the rest of your session. The next section of G-Land's reef, Launching Pads, is a good wave in itself, but it's generally used to set up G-Land's ultimate tube section, Speed Reef. Speed Reef turns on when a wave bowls off of Launching Pads, doubles up, and heaves on a freakily shallow reef, offering a deep and "speedy" barrel all the way into the bay. Speedies is the most shallow of all of G-Land's sections, but like most waves in the world, it also has the best inside view.

G-Land is as challenging as any wave in the world, and under the right conditions it is also the fastest. It requires a lot of experience in heavy waves as well as a lot of knowledge of equipment. Boards should be narrow, thick, and gunny, but not so long that they won't fit the cylindrical character of the G-Land barrel. The emphasis here is on gaining speed, managing a long ride, and getting shacked—not airs and single-blast maneuvers. A surfer will endure lots of paddling, lots of hold-downs, maybe a few reef cuts, and a lot of walking over jagged reefs in the sweltering heat. There's also jungle wildlife to contend with and the mosquitoes carry malaria. Booties, helmets, and anti-malarial medications are wise choices. There's no doubt that G-Land can place a variety of obstacles in your path—some challenging and others just leaving you to wonder if it's worth all the hassle. But one good barrel off Launching Pads and on through Speedies' end-section will make your entire trip.

Above: *A fortunate surfer paddles toward Grajagan—the heart of the Indonesian surf experience.*

Right: *Welcome to G-Land! Hope you like to ride freight train left tubes all day, because other than the wave, there's not much else to do here.*

Left: *Don't be fooled by this photo; there's no such thing as a "shoulder" at G-Land. Another screamer races down the appropriately named Speed Reef section.*

LAGUNDRI BAY, NIAS, INDONESIA

Though it has been somewhat eclipsed by the nearby and heavily frequented Mentawai Islands in the past decade, the machine-like point at Lagundri Bay off the island of Nias in southwestern Sumatra still remains one the best right-hand waves in all of Indonesia, if not the world.

Discovered in 1975, Nias is just like any other classic Indonesian surf spot—it is paradise. Only here, Eden is sweeter for regularfoots, this being one of the few right-hand options for power-hungry and pit-minded surfers. The village, or nowadays, town, at Lagundri Bay is now fully equipped with hotels and restaurants to comfort the many traveling surfers, and practically any need can be fulfilled. The place has become so accommodating in the last 25 years that there is often massive overcrowding in the water during peak, Southern Hemisphere dry season months. After all, even with a new conveyor belt of surfers heading to the Mentawais, this is still Nias—and the place still holds legendary status.

The main surfing focus at Nias is on The Point, a super-hollow, sucky barrel that lines up perfectly along the reef, retaining its size for the entire ride. For its power and shallowness, The Point is a rather easy tube to set up, and the potential for getting very, very deep inside and coming out dry is great, during cleaner southerly swells. Most tides are rideable here, especially on bigger swells. This wave doesn't offer much more than a barrel over six feet—not that there's anything wrong with that. After spitting, it shoulders off into a channel. However, cutting back at the wrong time or getting caught inside here is extremely hazardous, as the reef is quite bloodthirsty. Also, the wave's energy tends to suck one backward toward the peak, making it hard to get back to the channel. Under five feet, The Point can be a high-performance wave of epic proportions offering an endlessly smackable wall but, like most Indo reefbreaks, with smaller swells comes shallower water. Be prepared to break a surfboard or two here. Helmets and reef booties might keep you from breaking too much more.

Surfers must take heed here. The Point at Lagundri Bay is beautiful, glorious, and everything you imagined it can be. But don't be too hypnotized by it—it can wake you up in a most violent manner.

Above: *Many don't mind the ongoing development of the Lagundri Bay area. After all, air conditioning and room service sure beat malaria on the beach.*

Right: *While known more for its epic lefts, Indonesia has its share of rights too. Sumatra's Nias stands at attention.*

LAKEY PEAK, SUMBAWA, INDONESIA

Located two islands east of Bali, southeast Sumbawa's Lakai Beach boasts what is probably the most convenient setup in all of Indonesia outside of Bali. No fewer than six surf camps with all the amenities sit right out front of two world-class waves, with another waiting a little under a mile down the beach.

The main wave of the Lakai (or Lakey) region is Lakey Peak, one of the few split-peak reefbreaks in the Indonesian island chain. Lakey Peak is defined by a peak with a crisp, right-hand tube section and also a heavier and longer left throwing a perfectly round barrel. This spot can hold waves up to the ten-foot range, but it works best at four to six feet: conditions typically go downhill with any increase in size after ten feet here. Because most waves in Indo have a point-like quality to them, Lakey's prized A-frame makes it the most widely surfed wave in this area, and with the many surf camps on the shoreline, crowds can be a problem. Lower tides make this break shallower and much more dangerous, all but shutting down the right, but also serving to weed out some of the less-keen devotees.

Right to the left of Lakey Peak is the pleasantly nasty wave known as Lakey Pipe. An unpredictable left-hand barrel, Lakey Pipe closes out on bigger swells, but it's capable of throwing a barrel as good as any left at the Peak. If neither of these waves does it for you, a short walk farther down the coast will bring you to Periscope Point. Periscope is a long right-hand reef-point with a frustratingly narrow swell window. It is still world-class, but under much more constricted perimeters. This wave requires proper cooperation from the trades, as wind conditions are vital to its success. The wave at Periscope offers several tight barrels—two or three on one wave sometimes—but due to its fickle nature, it can turn off instantly, leaving those who took the walk to wonder where it all went. This reef can also get painfully dry at times.

While Lakey's might not be the best bet for an Indonesian excursion, it tends to be more consistent than G-Land throughout the year, as it often breaks with good winds in the off-season, which is the Southern Hemisphere summer. And given the many breaks that lie within walking distance of each other, Lakey's could be the finest ingredient to an Indian Ocean odyssey.

Above: *A distant view of Sumbawa's Lakey, yet another island-hopping alternative in Indonesia and surfing's ultimate amusement park.*
Right: *Lakey Peak offers one of the few spit-peak experiences in Indonesia. And with the crowds frequenting the place, it needs both of those directions.*

LANCE'S, SUMATRA, INDONESIA

Once the magic of Indonesia's Mentawai Islands—located off the west coast of Sumatra—was exposed to the public, surfers flocked in record numbers to the area. One of the most spellbinding waves in the Mentawais grabbing surfers' attention was Lance's Right, one of the few right-hand alternatives in a country of mostly lefts. Since professional surfers, industry people, traveling soulmen, and everyday Joes all wanted a crack at this amazingly hollow wave, it became the first spot in the Mentawais to show the ugly face of overcrowding—strange, considering this is one of the most primitive ends of the earth.

Lance's, also called H.T.'s, takes energy from the southern Indian Ocean and refracts it off a large offshore lava reef. The wave starts as a pitching barrel and—depending on a variety of factors, including swell fetch, tide, and size—will either break a little farther out, allowing for a smoother take-off and a barrel that's easier to set up, or suck out right from the start, making for late take-offs and sometimes disastrous reef floggings. Under the right conditions, Lance's Right is the most perfect barrel imaginable. Picture the best part of a wave, and keep that spinning cylinder's shape but move it along the reef at different speeds, sometimes forcing a rider to gun for his life, and other times allowing him to cut back into the juice. That's Lance's Right. There's also a left-hander around the headland from Lance's called Lance's Left, which is generally a more workable wave. Although this break offers a few nasty barrels, Lance's Right takes most of the attention off this otherwise fine left. Lance's Right can be ridden up to a large size, bigger than double-overhead, and may require bigger boards than what Indo breaks usually call for. Even helmets can be useful here sometimes. The reef at Lance's is dangerously shallow, so don't be fooled by the utter perfection of the wave itself. Lance's Right also breaks small, and it's one of the most rippable waves anywhere under the six-foot range with tubes, shoulders, and an endlessly boostable bowl.

As with most spots in the Mentawais, weather can be very unpredictable. Breezes off the Sumatran mainland might bless the area with offshores all day. Other times, quick-forming storms conveniently known as "Sumatras" might blow in across the Mentawai Strait, wrecking conditions at spots until it moves away. In fact, the fluctuating weather patterns may be the only thing deterring some surfers from visiting this highly publicized surfing destination. While boat charters in the area continue to battle each other for exclusivity rights to the breaks of the Mentawais, it's doubtful attention will lessen on the area anytime soon.

Below left: *A rare beach view of Lance's Right. If you find yourself on the shore, hurry up and get back in the water. Many of Indonesia's islands are plagued by malaria-carrying mosquitoes.*

Below: *Lance's Right, located in Indonesia's Mentawai Islands, is one of the more popular stops for photo-hungry pros, and good sessions here rarely go down nowadays without the complete entourage.*

MACARONIS, SUMATRA, INDONESIA

While the swell-endowed Indonesian archipelago offers a variety of world-class lefts, including Desert Point, G-Land, and Padang Padang. Macaronis—situated inside a bay in the Mentawai Islands, a little more than 50 miles off the Sumatran coast—may be the best of them all. If it isn't the best, then it's certainly one of them, and it's definitely the most user-friendly. Not to say Macaronis doesn't have its own hazards. The reef can get very shallow here at different points, the sun is even more intense than in Bali, and malaria poses a constant threat to any surfer—particularly one who ventures landward. But the setup of the wave itself at Macaronis is truly magnificent, and the emphasis here is more on high-performance ripping rather than testing fate.

When Macaronis is breaking in all its spinning glory, it can be the most rippable wave in the world, featuring multiple barrel sections and a long wall made for high-speed banks, long floaters, cutbacks, airs, and anything else a surfer can devise. With such an insanely long, bending bowl, this break can get crowded, too, although the sheer length of the wave helps to make it seem less so.

The Macaronis take-off zone can be tight, as it doesn't tend to shift as much as other Mentawai breaks, like Lance's. This left breaks all the way across a bending lava shelf, and is best at six or seven feet. Any bigger and sections might mush out. This wave is also heavily photographed and videoed and its magic has been brought to the public time and time again in magazines and surf celluloid. Macaronis is both a wave to practice for, and a wave to practice on. Surfers of almost any skill level will feel zmore comfortable surfing here than at other, more challenging Indonesian breaks like G-Land or Nias, and despite the threat of other charters bringing more surfers to the lineup, a good session at Macaronis will make your trip worthwhile.

The main season for surf in the Mentawais is the Southern Hemisphere winter, which is also the dry season. This is when offshore winds are far more likely. Monsoon weather typically occurs throughout the rest of the year, often bringing with it terrible winds and all-day downpours. One of the best things about the Mentawais though, is that since they're such small islands—many of which are still sinking into the ocean—one break can be onshore, and a little way around the bend there can be a perfect reef holding overhead swell in offshore conditions. Go exploring—that is, if you can talk the boat captain into it.

Above and right: *Perfect tube, perfect wall, and perfect air sections creates a perfect wave.*

PADANG PADANG, BALI, INDONESIA

Made popular in the '70s by such traveling legends as Gerry Lopez and Peter McCabe, Bali's Bukitan Peninsula quickly earned the reputation as the fantasy land of all fantasy lands with its series of flawless left-hand reefbreaks. The Bukit's heaviest spot, Padang Padang, while cursed with the cheesy reputation of being "so good you have to name it twice," is also the sketchiest, most ruthless wave on the entire island of Bali.

Located right down the road from Impossibles, another classic left, Padang Padang heaves on a shallow patch of reef close to a jagged cliff. Depending on the tide and direction of the swell, the wave will either be an instant tube from the start or a long, workable bowl allowing the rider to make a few crucial pumps before pulling into a deeper barrel down the line. Though this spot is commonly referred to as "The Balinese Pipeline," Padang Padang is much less peaky than its gnarlier cousin, and it generally offers a longer ride. Several coverups on one wave is an ordinary occurrence. Giant foamballs can prove to be an obstacle on set-waves, warping an otherwise perfect bowl. The wave at Padang usually allows the fastest surfers enough face room in between tube sections to execute a few off-the-tops. Riders must kick out before the wave's end, though, as it sucks out over a creepily dry section of coral. Padang Padang starts to break around five feet at its smallest, making it hard to work one's way up. Basically, it's either mental or it's flat. It's best to ride this place at mid-tide, as the reef can get a little too close for comfort during lower tides.

The crowds, often mostly composed of Australians, can get very thick when Padang Padang is going off. You must be a skilled and experienced tube-rider to crack this break, and the local Balinese will gladly show you how it's done. Be ready to witness some phenomenal surfing. This is one of the most dangerous waves in all of Indonesia, and its ferocity is masked by its crystalline lip lines and blue-green-blue waters. If you're looking for a challenging wave, but one not quite as deadly, plenty of other spots along the Bukit might be more easily ridden and less crowded, and have a deeper bottom than Padang Padang. The lineup here on good swells is tense and aggressive, souring an otherwise soulful Indonesian adventure.

Booties are a must here, as in all of Indonesia. Although you may not need them, you're always better with them just in case. Reef cuts are almost a guaranteed certainty here, but some say just one cool, green barrel at Padang Padang is worth the Neosporin.

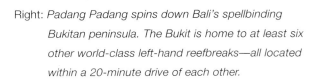

Right: *Padang Padang spins down Bali's spellbinding Bukitan peninsula. The Bukit is home to at least six other world-class left-hand reefbreaks—all located within a 20-minute drive of each other.*

ULUWATU, BALI, INDONESIA

Uluwatu is the most famous of all Balinese surf spots. Located at the southern tip of the Bukitan Peninsula, the spot's name translates as "evil waters" in Indonesian. The Balinese people, who are predominantly Hindu, believe the spirits of the sea can be malevolent around these seas. Yet while Uluwatu definitely has its share of the dangers that come with surfing—its sometimes offensively shallow reefs particularly—it still attracts more crowds than anywhere in Bali, most likely due to its rideability factor, easy access, and its almost played-out popularity.

Following the release of Albie Falzon's 1972 film, *Morning of the Earth*, surfers from everywhere, particularly nearby Australia, arrived in Bali to sample Uluwatu's dreamy left-hand magic. Nowadays, the waves certainly don't lack any of the same mystique. More often than not, once you paddle out through the cave heading the break, you'll see it's just like what has been pictured in the magazines for years—a sparkling-blue, draining reef-point. Besides the waves, the facilities lying atop the cliffs house some of the most surfer-friendly facilities anywhere in the world. It's possible to surf eight- to ten-foot barrels all morning, then come up here, get any dings fixed, and enjoy a meal and a full-body massage while you watch your buddies pull in deep below.

Emerging from the cave at Uluwatu, a surfer gets his first look at the wave's many sections. The Peak, Ulu's main section, is a nicely shaped wave at almost any size; thus it's one of the most dependable peaks to charge. And it draws in surfers by the truckload, causing tension in the lineup, particularly in the Southern Hemisphere winter when better swell conditions bring more people to Bali. The Peak breaks very rapidly on bigger swells, and only the fastest surfers—like the local Balinese—have the speed trim required to make the connection to the Racetracks section.

At its prime, Racetracks is a wonderfully round barrel that offers a wall to gain speed on, hence the name. A surfer will need that speed, since Racetracks soon drops out over extremely shallow reef, offering one of the throatiest barrels in all of Bali. Surfers should watch how far they ride this wave, as it gets very shallow, very quickly. Reef cuts are likely. But strangely, while Racetracks is the best part of Uluwatu, it's also probably the least crowded section, as many surfers are lured by the appeal of the Peak up the point.

Outside Corner is another section of Ulu's, which breaks with world-class shape, size, and power but shows its fury only on larger swells of eight feet plus. This wave is fairly rare and extremely challenging. When it's cranking, Outside Corner requires big-wave equipment, training, and courage. Temples, on the other hand, lies up the point from the rest of the breaks and offers a less life-threatening thrill on smaller swells. Almost anyone can surf this wave, and at six feet, it can be all the challenge some people want in Bali. Whatever peak you choose though, your first surf at Uluwatu will certainly not be your last. After all, there must be a reason why it's almost always crowded. Probably it's because it's almost always good.

Above: *Forget airs and tailslides. Surfing in Indonesia is all about speed and barrel-riding.*

Right: *Uluwatu, on Bali's Bukitan Peninsula, remains the island's most popular and most crowded surfbreak. One of the classic left reefpoints in the world, Ulu's rideability is rivaled only by its surrounding beauty.*

THE PACIFIC ISLANDS

These breaks—if they can be considered surfbreaks—
represent the ultimate test of a surfer's skill, testing not
only his physical ability, but also his emotional maturity
and his mental toughness. Pipeline, Cloudbreak,
Waimea, Teahupo'o—these waves aren't just heavy,
they're deadly. They're the biggest and baddest waves
in the world, breaking in the biggest, baddest ocean in
the world. Spots here are blessed by no fewer than four
different swell generators working at all times, a plethora
of currents, and fabulously sculpted, and usually
shallow reefs. Every year, legions of surfers answer the
call of the wild, intent on testing their mettle against the
roughest conditions known to man. Others avoid it.
Places like Teahupo'o and the North Shore draw a
deep-seated feeling of fear to the surface, and some
prefer to treat it like the monster in the closet—best not
to open that door. But a good ride at any of these
breaks can make all the danger seem meager in
comparison with the thrill. As any veteran of these
breaks will attest, these waves can change your life.
They can also take your life.

Right: *"But I thought Waimea was a right."* Despite its rideable
appearance here, the Waimea shorebreak remains the
least-desired route in from the spot.

HONOLUA BAY, MAUI, HAWAIII

While not as popular a surfing pilgrimage as the North Shore of Oahu, the island of Maui produces some of the best waves anywhere in the Hawaiian chain, supported by a far less intense vibe in its still dense, but mellower crowds. Its premier right-hander, Honolua, meaning "two harbors," is blessed with one of the most picturesque setups in all the world—beautiful, lush tropical fauna carving pristine valleys up volcanic cliffs over the Bay. The wave can be equally as breathtaking as the scenery, and the roping right-handers Honolua is famous for producing hold legendary status among many esteemed Hawaiian waveriders. The spot was a sideline destination for California's best surfers in the early '60s, but it wasn't until 1967, when Dick Brewer ran the Bay's first surf contest, that the rest of the surfing world outside Hawaii took an interest.

Honolua Bay is a long right-hand point offering several barrel sections under optimal conditions. The first section, Coconuts, breaks dangerously close to the cliffs on the inside before it makes its way into the Bay. There's a huge cave with a shallow, urchin-covered bottom waiting dead ahead, which can spell disaster if you eat it. The wave gets shallower and faster on the inside, but it often races too quickly for the rider to make the necessary connection. Honolua can be a fairly moody wave too. One day it might break as a four-foot, high-performance paradise, made for any combination of off-the-tops, sweeping cutbacks, and long floaters. Other times it will be a wide-open, thick-lipped, ten-by-ten-foot cavern where the rider can stand with his arms outstretched and never come close to touching any part of the cave's walls. While these latter days are fairly rare, many believe them well worth waiting for. The island of Molokai tends to block a lot of the energy coming from the North Pacific, so big, epic days are typically numbered here.

The right at Honolua Bay operates under the same swell required to make Waimea Bay break—a strong northwest, with more north than west. But although the size making it through here is generally half of what it would be on the North Shore, the winds are almost always calmer in the winter, as Honolua is better protected from the southerly "Kona" tradewinds. With an unruffled, sparkling-blue curl ahead, the inside-the-tube-looking-out view of Honolua is one of the most magical in surfing.

Surfing Honolua Bay is a far less stressful endeavor than on the North Shore. With the point-like quality of the waves, catching a set wave down the line is within almost any surfer's reach, but the serenity and idyllic wonder of the Honolua backdrop belies the heaviness of the wave. It may be Maui, not Oahu, but once you paddle out, the waves will quickly remind you where you are. You're in Hawaii. And Hawaii's always been a pretty place.

Above: *Maui's Honolua Bay offers one of the most idyllic backdrops in all the surfing world. The wave itself is very impressive too.*

Right: *Even in Hawaii, you can occasionally slip through the pack and snag a smaller one on the inside. Honolua Bay.*

MAKAHA POINT, OAHU, HAWAII

While hundreds of surfers scurry like roaches to the North Shore every winter in an attempt to prove themselves in front of the cameras, the locals of Makaha, on the Westside of Oahu, sit docile and happy in their beach chairs. Plucking ukeleles, roasting pigs, and holding luaus right on the beach, why wouldn't they? Their entire families are there, and their families' families, too. A half century since The Makaha International earned it worldwide acclaim, 60 years since it was considered the heaviest new frontier in the Hawaiian Islands, Makaha is still the place that embodies the Hawaiian spirit in its purest essence.

A deeply familial place, Makaha is made up of several simply named spots—The Point, The Bowl, The Blowhole, and The Inside Reef—all turning on with varying degrees throughout the years. The most revered wave, though, is Makaha Point. The Point breaks only when a long-interval pulse is too big for the North Shore to hold. When the proper forces align, giant northwest swells travel southward, wrapping around Kaena Point. And once in a while—once in a lifetime maybe—those swells form gargantuan, 20- to 40-foot monsters pitching off The Point, screaming through The Bowl, and ending in the channel. When it's big and it's on, Makaha Point is considered by some to be the longest big-wave spot in the world. What makes the break different from big-wave locales like Waimea Bay or Todos Santos is the infamous Bowl, a frighteningly unpredictable slab of ocean lining up to send even the best surfers in the world flying. After making the drop at The Point, the rider must take on The Bowl. Kicking out is not an option since the wave's moving so fast and a pantheon of sets are bound to be behind it. On days like this, Makaha is as big and scary as any wave in the world. In 1969, famous big-wave charger Greg "Da Bull" Noll almost drowned following a severe wipeout in what was estimated as being 45 to 50-foot Point surf. He was so shook up, in fact, he almost quit surfing and refused to discuss the experience for some time afterward. Classic, big days like these are rare in Makaha. In general, the place receives great wind conditions but not a whole lot of consistent, well-angled swells. Even more rare than giant Point surf is witnessing someone ride the wave successfully—from Point to channel. Those who perform this feat are given instant hero status and admittance into the elite group known as "The Point Screamers."

In her typical warmhearted light, the late Rell Sunn—The Queen of Makaha—started a contest in Makaha for locals before her death in 1998 to help pass on the Makaha surfing legacy to Westside groms. The 2000 Association of Surfing Professionals World Champion, Sunny Garcia, wears his Westside tag tattoo like a proud badge of courage wherever he goes in the world, and he vows to eventually settle down there with his family once his career has slowed down. Makaha has that kind of hold over people. While every other inch of Oahu seems to get more and more exploited by the day, Makaha still manages to keep it in the family.

Above: *Another screamer races down the point.*

Right: *Aloha and mahalo, from Makaha Point.*

PIPELINE, OAHU, HAWAII

The Banzai Pipeline. Here's a wave that totally transcends the sport. Songs have been recorded about it. Movies have been based on it. And more than a few people base their entire lives around it. Anyone who knows anything about surfing knows Pipeline is hands-down the largest, thickest, most unforgiving gladiator pit in all of creation. Those who ride it successfully enjoy god-like status. Those who don't sometimes die.

First charged in the early '60s, the wave at Pipeline is formed when large North Pacific swells, most ideally coming from the west or northwest during the Northern Hemisphere winter, strike a black lava reef. The more north the swell turns, the nastier the conditions get. Contrary to popular belief, the reef here isn't made of the same razor-sharp fire coral found in the South Pacific. The bottom is composed of a network of caves and boulders, and sand builds up against the reef in the summertime.

Pipe has three sections, the first being an inside reef operating from two to ten feet. This is what offers the classic Pipe setup—heaving lips crashing down, spinning a roomy barrel before flattening off into the channel. This is when the spot is also at its most hazardous, it being the shallowest Pipe setup. Second Reef starts at ten feet and is rideable up to 18 feet. Under these conditions, the take-off zone is easy to access, offering simple drops and a big wall to fade before the wave reforms and jacks on the inside. Third Reef is pretty much maxed-out Pipeline, breaking at twenty feet and bigger. The spot is rarely ridden, since it's so far out and chances are somewhere else will be better.

When Pipeline gets a west swell with a bit of north, it throws nice peaks and the infamous Backdoor starts to work. Backdoor is the right swinging off the Pipeline peak toward the narrow channel between the break and Off The Wall. It is unfathomably dangerous—some say more so than Pipe's front door—as it strikes the shallowest part of the reef. As a matter of fact, some claim Backdoor Pipeline is nothing more than a glorified closeout, and they may be right. Only

Above: *World Championship Tour surfer Shea Lopez gets in nice and early on a deceivingly deadly Pipe set.*

the world's best pros and the most in-tune locals know how to ride these racy bombs and make it back out to the lineup unscathed. Following a ride through Backdoor's bowels, you're looking right at Off The Wall, a bad place to be caught inside.

In general, a surfer needs a narrow pintail gun here, long and thick, but not too long so it won't pearl in Pipe's extreme bottom curves. The wave is best approached on a medium tide with the light southeast trades blowing offshore. Perhaps more than the oceanic conditions surrounding this surf spot, it's the crowd that makes it so dangerous. Pipeline has the most neck-to-neck lineup ever, not to mention a recognized pecking order. Collisions, vibings, and fistfights are everyday occurrences. The best waves are generally reserved for the A-team. As for the rest of the surfers sitting waiting for scraps, unfortunately, there isn't enough of Pipeline to go around on even the wimpiest days. After all, it is Pipeline—the most famous wave in the world. Always has been. And most likely, it always will be.

Below: *Robbie Page places a lot of faith in his edgework and equipment so he can get under the lip and to the safety of the shoulder at Oahu's Banzai Pipeline.*

ROCKY POINT, OAHU, HAWAII

Contrasting the death-before-dishonor attitude needed for charging the life-threatening mountains of water of the North Shore, the mid-size waves at Rocky Point—lying between Pupukea and Kammieland—are comparatively . . . fun. By far the most consistent spot on the North Shore, Rocky Point will break from one foot to eight on practically any given swell, any wind, or any tide, though it does tend to favor some conditions over others.

Marked by a curved reef more than 200 yards wide, Rocky provides surfers with everything from crisp tubes to smackable walls to catastrophic air sections. The hands-down high-performance barometer of Hawaii, several never-before-seen maneuvers were exposed to the surfing public here for the first time. For example, Taylor Steele's 1996 release *Good Times* featured the first full-rotation frontside 360 aerial, punted by Rocky's regular Kalani Robb off the end section. With such an emphasis on state-of-the-art surfing and an expansive playing field of smaller, rippable waves, this is often the only place for visiting pros to surf when the major spots are pushing maximum density—both in size and locals. During any heavily attended winter on the North Shore, there might be as many as 50 photographers and videographers on the shore at any given time— all hoping to snap a shot of that lofty air or spray-chucking carve. With that many media personnel on the beach, one gets a sense of how many surfers are sure to be out. And at Rocky's, every demographic and nationality is represented—Americans, Australians, Brazilians, groms, vets, locals, and so on.

North swells generally provide long walls with a few barrels here and there, but the waves are more prone to closeouts then too. On swells with more west, the epic Rocky's left begins to take shape—throwing a feathery wall and a ludicrous inside boost section, thrusting the rider into the wind and giving him the necessary stickage to pull off the incredible. Though somewhat of a playful wave, Rocky's does house a nasty reef below. They don't call it "Rocky" Point for nothing.

This spot was prone to a fair amount of localism in the '70s, but since the media has made it a mission to spend an exorbitant amount of their time shooting during their North Shore trips, things have calmed down a bit. Now the lineup is so scattered, so diverse, and so not worth fighting about, surfers pretty much keep to their own program. Besides, if you throw a lot of bad vibes—or worse, a fist— not only will your misdeeds most likely be caught by every video camera and 600-mm lens this side of Cape Hatteras, but you'll probably miss that punchy left heading your way, begging to be obliterated. Remember, you're here for the surf—not the turf.

Above: *Richard Cram lays down a backside bottom turn on a bigger set at Rocky Point. If it is this heavy here, you can count on other North Shore spots being outright mammoth.*

Left: *A clean day at Rocky Point. Not exactly Pipeline or Waimea, but certainly it's better than your average day at the shorebreak.*

Below: *Derek Ho gives new definition to the term "riding shotgun" as he shoots through this juicy Rocky left.*

SUNSET BEACH, OAHU, HAWAII

Perhaps the world's most complex setup, Sunset Beach lies on a plane far removed from any other in our sport. Just sitting in the lineup is a massive test of endurance, mental toughness, and ocean awareness. Cleanup sets, nightmare rips, a sudden, bottom-dropping inside bowl, and the notoriously dangerous West Peak—there are a million ways to get seriously injured or even killed at Sunset Beach, and you almost never see any of them coming.

Though the popularity of the spot has been somewhat diluted in decades past, Sunset made a massive encore appearance in the Association of Surfing Professionals World Tour in 2001. Deciding the most dramatic title chase in pro surfing history, involving no fewer than eight contenders, Sunset Beach was the concluding event, a slot normally reserved for the more in-your-face spectacle of Pipeline. This time, though, the once-famous proving ground for early North Shore pioneers was once again center stage. Located between Kammieland Reef and Sunset Point, the wave at Sunset is an enigma in itself. Giant lava fingers beckoning out to sea cause giant A-frame peaks to form. Ideally, Sunset Beach needs a west swell to truly work its magic. Breaking from a pretty good size to downright monstrous, Sunset is best at ten to 12 feet, with southeast trades blowing lightly offshore.

The wave is composed of three parts. On smaller swells, Sunset Point will break up to six feet, but it is extremely difficult to get a good one, as it's often little more than a sporadic series of chunks. Sunset's main reef breaks from eight feet all the way up to 15 feet when conditions are right. Being an open-ocean wave, Sunset is drastically affected by the tiniest change in environmental stimuli. Too much north and the wave will be bumpy and unpredictable. A barrel might open up at these times, but it will be almost impossible to read. On a west swell, there's generally a steeper drop and a more definitive peak. Whatever the conditions, one must be prepared for everything

Above: *Sunset Beach lives up to its name. Some surfers are still enjoying the surf here at dusk.*

the North Pacific can dish out here. One of the worst things that can happen to you in your surfing career is getting caught inside by a West Peak at Sunset. The currents will drag you right to the center of the explosion, blasting you underwater all the way to the inside, where your problems just begin. Although it's an experts-only wave when macking, it's best for all surfers to check out the lineup before paddling out. Then after getting out, it's best to sit and watch the surfers who know the place. Then, just to be safe . . . go in and try it the next day.

The point is, you can never be too careful at Sunset Beach. Blustery trades blowing up the face make hard take-offs even harder. The rips will toss you around like salad, and the A-team crowd consists of a bunch of locals who know what they're doing and can't wait to call you out for not knowing what you're doing. If you really want it, go out and get it, but remember—more so than with any other break—patience is a virtue at Sunset Beach.

Below, inset: *Sunset Beach remains one of the most complicated lineups in the world to master, and those who ride it well are considered watermen of the highest degree.*

Below: *Cheyne Horan drops into a thick peak at Sunset Beach, the North Shore's crown jewel. Think this looks difficult? This is the easy part. Wait until he gets to the inside.*

TAVARUA, FIJI

Tavarua is the ultimate beach resort. Located in an idyllic Fijian dreamscape, this small island boasts a variety of ocean-oriented activities—one of which just happens to be surfing some of the best waves on the planet. Lying just to the west of Viti Levu, Tavarua, on the island of Fiji, the Tavarua Surf Camp and its three heavenly surf spots—Tavarua Rights, Restaurants Reef, and Cloudbreak—has what can be a dreadfully long reservation list to get on, often taking as long as years, but after two decades, this place remains the quintessential surf resort, admitting no more than 24 surfers on the island at any time: paradise in a world of otherwise crowd soured surfbreaks.

A one-mile boat ride to the south of the island, Cloudbreak—Tavarua's most majestic wave—lies at the corner of a giant reef pass taking the brunt of Southern Hemis marching across the Pacific. Being in the open ocean, these swells hit Cloudbreak's outer section with speed to burn, and surfers are often forced to stroke for their lives just to get into it. The inside section, dubbed "Shishkabobs" for its shallow, skewer-like coral heads, poses the greatest threat to surfers. Plenty of skin has been left here over the years, as Cloudbreak can take unruly swells and distribute their energy in strange, unreadable ways. Sometimes the place offers long, workable walls in the head-high range with high-pocket tubes, and other times it mutates into a thick, ledgy double-up, and heaves triple-overhead mammoths violently on the reef. Wave selection and timing is everything at Cloudbreak. Sometimes it calls for stalling, other times fading, and other times gunning for daylight.

There are two other waves worth mentioning on the island. Tavarua Rights, located on the southeastern end, is an excellent off-season wave. It is also quite fickle and requires a properly directed cyclone swell to pass. Restaurants Reef, named for the restaurant in front of it, is a super-rippable left-hander that offers several deep tube sections and a seemingly endless lip line. But Restaurants can be

Above: *Tavarua, Fiji, is a place where you can have your cake and eat it too. The waves? That's the icing.*

painfully shallow on smaller swells, especially at low tide, and its size is usually half of what awaits at Cloudbreak. The prime season for Cloudbreak is the Southern Hemisphere winter, and tradewinds here usually blow in from the southeast, giving Cloudbreak offshore conditions most mornings.

Cloudbreak's reef can be as shallow as any pass in the world and bacterial infections are common, so all wounds should be cleaned thoroughly. Also, as in most tropical destinations, the sun is your enemy. However, one aspect of surfing that's pleasantly absent from Cloudbreak, and all of Tavarua's breaks, is localism. Dave Clark and Scott Funk obtained surfing rights to the break from the Fijian government in 1984 and set up shop here. Before you dismiss the idea of private ownership of the world's surf spots, keep this in mind: Everyone in the lineup at Cloudbreak takes turns going on waves. When was the last time you saw that on a surf trip?

Below: *Tuned in like only a local can be, transplanted Tavarua boat driver Jon Roseman regularly gets the best waves to hit Cloudbreak.*

TEAHUPO'O, TAHITI

Tahiti is the source of some of the most spellbinding waves to ever grace the pages of surf magazines. Sitting smack-dab in the middle of French Polynesia in the South Pacific Ocean, the archipelago's surf spots—some of which are yet to be discovered—redefine both perfection and terror. "The End of the Road" was the name first given to a certain Tahitian break occupying a reef pass at the edge of the extinct Passa Hava'e volcano. When witnessing this folding monstrosity's fury, though, "End of the Road" sounds more fitting compared with what we currently know the break as—Teahupo'o.

If Teahupo'o isn't the heaviest, most lethal wave on the planet, it's definitely running a close second or third. Since its shallow, fire-coral reef confronts prevailing southwest swells, formed by the Roaring Forties, dead on, South Pacific juice has nowhere to go but underneath itself, forming a lip that's thicker than the wave is tall. However, this is a wave that has to be measured in the negatives, since it literally breaks below sea level. The ride at Teahupo'o is a short one, allowing for nothing but a barrel and possibly a cutback or two before it implodes on dry reef. It is, however, the most exhilarating ride you'll ever take.

Though the wave breaks in the same patch of reef every time, its entry zone is surprisingly small, maybe 60 or 70 yards in all, forcing a surfer straight into the pit every time. Strangely, a shoulder drop can be equally as dangerous as rushing the bowels, because the extreme hook of the wave makes for more vertical take-offs, not to mention you're closer to the reef there. On any swell bigger than six feet, this wave gets very serious.

It's best to catch Teahupo'o during the Southern Hemisphere winter. From November to April, the area is pounded by horrible weather and winds, and swells are also not nearly as consistent. Forget bringing your shortboard to tackle Teahupo'o. A gun is an absolute necessity, but it can't be too long, because the extreme squareness of the trough might cause the nose to pearl. The most important thing to surfing Teahupo'o is getting under the lip. If you must choose between a board that paddles well and a board that rides well, take the one that paddles better.

Crowds are the least of your worries here, as the locals are some of the best-natured, most surf-stoked people you'll ever see on an island. Tahiti reminds many surfers of what the North Shore of Oahu might have been like before overdevelopment took over. Bacterial infections caused by live coral slicings, the blazing Tahitian sun, and tiger sharks cruising the vicinity are, however, not so kind. Your biggest adversary at Teahupo'o, though, will be the wave itself. Gathering the gumption to take that first drop is half the battle.

It cannot be stressed enough that this is one of the most deadly waves anywhere, rideable for madmen and experts only, and its incredibly concentrated power must be respected. Days prior to the 2000 Gotcha Tahiti Pro, local surfer Briece Taerea lost his life following a ghastly wipeout here, placing an ominous shadow over a surfbreak with an already dark reputation.

Above: *Teahupo'o—a wave so awesome, sometimes you have to paddle away from it.*

Right: *A bulbous barrel throws out so wide at Tahiti's Teahupo'o, you could almost drive a bus through it.*

WAIMEA BAY, OAHU, HAWAII

Off Kam Highway in Waimea Beach Park lies the great granddaddy of all big-wave arenas, Waimea Bay. This spot's history is as thick as its lips. Greg "Da Bull" Noll rode the first wave there in 1957, and since then it has become a fitting barometer for a waterman's knowledge, commitment, and courage. Even with the current tow-in phenomenon earning its place in the spectrum, not to mention darker, sharkier waves popping up in various corners of the world, Waimea still has more history and lore behind it than any other big-wave break—ever. And it still holds its own against any in terms of ferocity.

The classic Waimea setup is formed when a northwest swell strikes a pothole-indented, black lava shelf lying deep below the surface. The sheer mass of this wave is enough to kill most of those who attempt it, and riders here are required to be in peak physical condition and be one with their equipment. Many of Waimea's best watermen spend months training for that one special day. This is one spot where experience and ocean knowledge far surpass athletic skill and determination. Not to say a big dose of those two ingredients isn't needed as well, it's just that Waimea Bay truly represents what Hawaiian big-wave surfers are all about. When a decent 25 foot swell hits the bay during its waiting period, "The Eddie"—officially called "The Quiksilver in Memory of Eddie Aikau"—is held here in memory of Waimea's long-lost favorite son. This event is perhaps the most prestigious of any surf contest in the world and just getting invited, even as an alternate, is an honor in itself.

Like Todos Santos, the wave face at The Bay is marked by huge boils that are capable of dragging a person under the water and literally shooting them toward shore. The waves are immense, the currents are beyond treacherous, and the only way to the beach is through the east end of The Bay. If you miss that spot, which isn't difficult to do, you then must paddle all the way around the length of The Bay or attempt to make it in through the shorebreak. The shorebreak is formed when northwest winds push the sand in, and it can, has, and will snap a surfer's bones like toothpicks quicker than he can say, "Going left."

So with all the potentially life-threatening elements, what makes Waimea worth it? Most will attest to it being the drop. The drop is what keeps surfers coming back. For many big-wave heroes, nowhere is the adrenaline more intense than taking a few extra strokes before dropping over that voluminous ledge. At Waimea, although you may feel alone when plummeting over the falls into oblivion or racing off the bottom for the shoulder, you're not alone. No one is. All the surfers who made themselves legends there are watching. Eddie's watching. God is watching.

Above: *These guys can't afford to have their guns misfire. They prepare to psych-up at Waimea Bay, Oahu's big-wave Mecca.*

Left: *Waimea shorebreak is somewhat rideable on smaller swells—for the clueless and the insane.*

Below: *Two surfers split a wave at Waimea Bay. Here, Hawaiians sharing rides are a common sight. But that doesn't mean you should go out and follow suit.*

North America is at the heart of global surf culture. Nearly every company with ties to waveriding is based here, 20 world champions call it home, and this is also where a majority of surf media giants are headquartered. The continent wasn't the birthplace of the sport, but from the day the first waves were ridden along its west coast, North America has certainly been the leading catalyst for surfing's growth. And of course the continent wouldn't be worth a bar of wax if it didn't possess epic waves. Stuck between two of the planet's roughest oceans, North America houses two vast and distinctive coastlines with hundreds of world-class breaks. And just to the east and south, the Bahamas and Caribbean Islands offer North Americans easy access to dozens of idyllic tropical lineups as well. Although every year the region's residents spend thousands of dollars traveling the globe in search of waves, North American and Caribbean surfers have everything they need right in their own backyards.

Right: *Who ever would have thought a wave this magnificent would lie less than an hour off the East Coast of the United States? Then again, given the Bahamas' favorable positioning, smack-dab in the center of Hurricane Alley, why wouldn't it?*

BLACK'S BEACH, CALIFORNIA

Southern California's legions of logo-emblazoned surfers hogging every conceivable bump in the Pacific can force even the most patient surfer into hiding. After all, most of the area's best breaks are nothing more than polluted, glorified windchops most of the time, right? There are more grommets and longboarders per square foot than at any trade show or pig pickin' on the coast, right? And there's always some tweaker waiting right around in the parking lot to rip off your stuff, right? Not if you're a Black's Beach surfer.

San Diego County's Black's Beach is the best beachbreak in the United States—a roaring, voluminous, board-breaking, life-flashing wave capable of separating your board from your leash and your head from your shoulders. A longtime nudist colony, the area used to be known more for its extremities than its extremes. The wave at Black's is somewhat of a phenomenon in the way of sand-bottomed breaks. A deepwater canyon lies just offshore, sucking in almost any type of west swell. Northwest and southwest swells both work here, but a straight south won't cut it. Black's wave can be one of the most fun imaginable when it's small, and it's a dream when it's head-high and clean. But it's also capable of holding size up to triple-overhead, and more often than not, it will be the biggest surfbreak in Southern California.

Black's throws both left and right peaks all along the beach just like any sand-bottomed place, but the beach's unique angle tends to make the lefts hollower and more lined-up. Basically, there are three peaks at Black's: North Peak, Middle Peak, and South Peak, their conditions varying with changes in swell and tide. Winter is the best time to try to score good Black's, as there are frequent northwest swells and there is more of a chance for the famed Santa Ana winds to groom conditions.

Crowds are always present here, but it's more spread out than most Southern California breaks. And when it's doing its thing, the sheer power and mass of Black's heaviest slabs helps keep the numbers down to only the most serious waveriders. Rip currents can be deadly, and more than one surfer has drowned here in recent years. Cleanup sets serve to do just that—"cleaning up" all the surfers

who don't belong in the widowmaking conditions. There are several different paths one can take down the steep cliffs to get to the beach, the one to the north being the one where you'll most likely see naked hippie dudes with glow sticks. Like many things in California, you just have to ignore the peripheral, and focus on that first glorious ride.

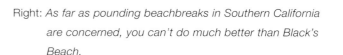

Right: *As far as pounding beachbreaks in Southern California are concerned, you can't do much better than Black's Beach.*

CAPE HATTERAS LIGHTHOUSE, NORTH CAROLINA

The swell-drenched barrier islands of the Outer Banks are a legitimate surfing oasis on an otherwise wave-starved coast. Dubbed "The Graveyard of the Atlantic" for all the vessels that have sunk throughout history off the Banks' weathered coastline, the Diamond Shoals located to the south side even served as a hangout for the infamous pirate Blackbeard in the 1700s. Folklore aside, though, this Atlantic graveyard comes to life when the surf picks up, and it has no shortage of devotees looking to grab some of its treasures.

Cape Hatteras lies at the southern end of the barrier island chain, and since the swell-diminishing continental shelf sits just off-shore, the power and size of the waves breaking here is almost always greater than on any other beach receiving a similar swell. Also, the beaches get brushed by two currents—the Labrador passing from the north, and the Gulf Stream passing from the south—making water temperatures fluctuate, sometimes dramatically, in mid-season. Though Cape Hatteras Lighthouse is the most renowned spot on the island, it's not always the greatest break. Sandbars are constantly shifting on the Outer Banks, and to find the best break during any given swell requires a bit of luck, and a lot of driving. In general, beaches along the northern Outer Banks like Duck, Kitty Hawk, and Nags Head allow for better conditions on north swells, and beaches farther south like Avon, Hatteras, and Frisco turn on with the souths. Whether it's the Cape Hatteras Lighthouse, which still serves as the home of the Eastern Surfing Association Championships despite the beacon itself being removed years ago, or some other sandbar to the north or south, all waves here are marked by the same characteristics—crunching beachbreak barrels, comparable in shape and power to Hossegor, France, or small-scale Puerto Escondido. Good swells can come at any time of the year, depending on a number of factors from the positioning of the jet stream to the unpredictable track of low pressure systems. The late Northern Hemisphere summer and fall are almost a sure thing, however, since that is the Atlantic tropical season. A hurricane swell in Hatteras can either be the best surfing conditions you have ever surfed, or, if the wind doesn't cooperate, just plain awful.

Lying in the humid subtropical zone of the continental United States, the water here is warm enough for just baggies in the summer but requires a fullsuit, booties, gloves, and sometimes even a hood in the winter.

At the Hatteras Lighthouse, localism can get hairy—particularly in the summer when the tourist boom is in full effect—but the vibe is generally less intense as the off-season approaches. Besides, if one spot on the Outer Banks is packed, another sandbar can be cranking right down the beach somewhere, and no one might know anything about it. Go searching, and you just might find your own graveyard waiting for one lucky surfer to bring it to life.

Above: *Conveniently positioned close to the Atlantic's swell-sapping continental shelf, North Carolina's Outer Banks are blessed with the most powerful beachbreaks on the East Coast. Bob Irazari leans into the power at Cape Hatteras.*

Right: *Don't get too attached to these Outer Banks homes in the photo. Located directly in harm's way come the Atlantic hurricane season, they might be washed out to sea by the next storm.*

Right, inset: *Local boy Jesse Hines gets a bit of pop off one of the Banks' bowly sections.*

INDICAS, ELBOW CAY, BAHAMAS

The Bahamas are often cursed by surfers, but rarely praised. This cluster of tiny islands blocks quite a bit of swell from reaching the coast of Florida, often making flat spells seem like an eternity for Sunshine State surfers. But within a short plane ride from the coast is one of the Caribbean's best-kept secrets—waves. The Bahamas are loaded with a variety of reefbreaks, beachbreaks, and points, some perfectly angled to produce unreal surfing conditions. The Abacos typically get the best the Bahamas has to offer. And Indicas, a firing left-hander, is the top spot in the Abacos.

In the winter, the Abacos receive consistent swells—usually in the three- to eight-foot range. In the summer, swells are less frequent, but conditions can be surprisingly fun—especially considering what Florida's beaches will typically look like. It does not offer as exhilarating an experience as can be found in other Caribbean haunts like Puerto Rico or Barbados, but what's striking about the Bahamas is that it's so close to the United States, seeming almost like an extension of the East Coast. From Florida, a surfer can get there in a little over two hours.

When faced with flat conditions in the southeast, it's hard to imagine the Bahamas would offer anything special. But the Abacos receive swell from nearly every direction, although the winds may or may not choose to cooperate. The reef at Indicas, like most Abacos breaks, is composed of live fire coral. Indicas breaks hard and hollow over this bottom, heaving one of the roundest barrels in the Caribbean when it's on. The wave tends to break like a shorebreak, with double-up sections on the inside. Indicas holds up to twelve-foot swells, or bigger on occasion, but it is generally best at head-high to a few feet overhead. Easterly winds work best, but the wave can be somewhat fun on bad winds as well.

To get there you will need to take a ferry from Marsh Island to the Abacos and you can stay right on the break, since it is located in front of a series of hotels. Another wave to check out is Garbonzos, which is a fabulous reefbreak that is more consistent, yet less sketchy than Indicas.

The rock dance over urchins and fire coral to many of these breaks can be nerve-racking, but at Indicas, or any break in the Abacos, the dreamy setup alone will have been worth the trip. And if your timing is good and you're lucky enough to catch it, you then might find yourself a lifetime Bahamas fan, praising the place instead of cursing it.

Above and Right: *If you catch the right swell in the Bahamas, you could find yourself enjoying the ride of your life.*

LOWER TRESTLES, CALIFORNIA

Not all our dream spots are rifling, muscle-cramping points or bone-crunching barrels. Sometimes the perfect wave is nothing more than a crisp line that allows a surfer to free his mind and ride to the best of his ability—and sometimes even beyond that. In the United States, and possibly the entire world, no surfbreak defines "rippable" better than the Southern California skate park known as Lower Trestles.

Lowers is a super-consistent, super-dependable, super-fun, point-like A-frame that breaks over a sand and cobblestone bottom. The nearby free-flowing San Mateo Creek deposits sediment into the waters of the break, helping to stabilize the world-class sandbars waiting just offshore for the slightest southerly pulse. While all of Trestles's waves—including Uppers, Cotton's, and Churches—offer their own separate little slices of heaven on a variety of tides and swells, nowhere can a surfer make use of their entire arsenal as at Lowers. The wave represents a crucial chapter in high-performance surf history. Aerial wizard Christian Fletcher, from San Clemente, California, almost single-handedly legitimized the aerial movement off the launchable lefts in the '80s, six-time World Champion Kelly Slater debuted his clinic on 21st Century Flow with a devastating display of carving 360s and tailsliding reverses on the rights in the 1991 Body Glove Surf Bout, and New Smyrna Beach, Florida's, Aaron "Gorkin" Cormican pulled the first-ever "Gorkin Flip"—a variation of snowboarding's Rodeo Flip—on a left-hander here in 2000. Who knows what people will be doing at Lowers in 2010?

In general, depending on the swell, the lefts wrapping toward Uppers tend to be bowly and have more boostable sections, while the right resembles a point perfect for long floaters and roundhouses. Working best during south and southwest swells, Lowers goes off during the Northern Hemisphere summer. Don't be put off by all the kids on summer vacation running down the trail to the break. They're the least of your worries when it comes to the crowds. After all, if it's good—and chances are it will be—every conceivable demographic is represented in the Trestles lineup: shortboarders, longboarders, kneeboarders, teenyboppers, ex-pros, current pros . . . you get the picture.

Although Lowers is a split peak from the start, the take-off zone is extremely tight, and there's a drop-in nearly every wave. And although you might fit in ten maneuvers on a single wave, you might get only two of those waves in three hours, so if it seems reasonable to you, charge it.

The good news, though, is that if you do get a bomb at Lowers—be it by quietly sitting far away from the peak and lucking into one that swings wide, or snaking a Mohawked, tattooed local on the set of the day—it will make you feel like a pro. And if you get enough practice on a wave like Lowers, you just might become one.

Above: *Believe it or not, this isn't even a crowded day by Lower Trestles standards. Lower is Southern California's performance pressure cooker, and sharing the experience with a few hundred unfamiliar faces is the ordinary.*

Right: *San Clemente's favorite son Christian Fletcher is the undisputed king of the frontside aerial—a move he perfected off the Lowers' launching pad.*

MANASQUAN INLET, NEW JERSEY

With the smash popularity of HBO's Mafia drama *The Sopranos*, the state of New Jersey has garnered the reputation as the headquarters for America's most famous organized crime family. And although this belief is purely Hollywood hype, there's absolutely no fabrication surrounding the fact that Jersey's Manasquan Inlet is a godfather among East Coast surfbreaks. Although Sebastian Inlet, Florida, is better known, Manasquan is probably the East Coast's best inlet in terms of overall quality. Regardless of which spot can claim to be top dog, this Jersey surfbreak definitely gets heaps of respect from everyone who's ever seen it flash its guns.

With a very similar setup to Sebastian, Manasquan breaks much the same as its Sunshine State counterpart. The main peak lies next to a long, rubble-mound jetty bordering the Manasquan River, which separates the towns of Manasquan and Point Pleasant. The lengthy jetty causes a refraction in the waves and thus an increase in their size and quality, and because this process can bump up a rideable swell in an almost flat ocean, expect the 'Squan to be the most consistent spot in the area. The wave itself is primarily a right-hander and is a little more peaky than the Florida wave, but also quite a bit longer. Taking off next to the jetty, it's not uncommon for surfers to ride nearly a hundred yards down the beach as the wave reels along toward another smaller groin to the north. Down the beach from the main peak, numerous quality A-frame setups offer both rights and lefts with insane inside bowl sections throwing out gaping pits over the extremely shallow sandbars.

The spot's best swells arrive from the southeast, and when huge hurricane lines hit the jetty, one advantage Manasquan has over its Sunshine State cousin quickly becomes evident—size. Although most years the break tops out at ten feet, Manasquan Inlet has held its form and been ridden up to 15 feet.

Jersey may get big, but it also gets cold. With water temps dropping into the 40s and even 30s during the winter, the place requires a ¾ mm fullsuit, gloves, and hoods for the coldest months. However, these harsh conditions breed an ultra hard-core bunch that has developed its own little crew called the Manasquan Inlet Cult.

Above: *A taste of Jersey juice at Manasquan Inlet.*
Right: *Despite the cold water, New Jersey locals still manage to cut loose. John Flynn gaffs the right off the rocks at Manasquan.*

These locals regulate the lineup at all times, especially when it gets crowded, which can be quite often. So when you paddle out at Manasquan, show the group and their home waters some courtesy and respect and you just might get some waves.

Below: *Jeff Beverly looking down the barrel of Manasquan's main gun.*

MAVERICKS, CALIFORNIA

Mavericks. The name alone strikes fear and awe into the hearts of surfers everywhere. The Northern California big-wave spot was almost completely unknown until the place gained headline status in the early to mid-'90s through a combination of surf magazine articles and the highly publicized death of Hawaiian pro Mark Foo. Ever since then, Mavs has been religiously covered by the media, become the leading challenge for almost every big-wave surfer, and even received its own specialty contest. Because of all this hype and the fact that this fearsome reefbreak boasts some of the planet's largest surf, Mavericks has evolved into the most famous heavy-water spot in the world, and in the process, it has changed the way in which we look at big-wave surfing.

A large part of the reason Mavericks has had such an effect on the sport lies in its inhospitable location. Unlike previous big-wave meccas like Waimea Bay, whose picture-perfect island atmosphere and tropical water temperatures make riding life-threatening surf seem downright appealing, Mavs is situated south of San Francisco in Half Moon Bay, right inside some of California's coldest and most shark-filled waters. Full wetsuits, hoods, and booties are the norm, and in just the past few years, two great white attacks have occurred on surfers and their watercraft at Mavericks. But the sharks and the cold are minor annoyances compared with the waves themselves.

Breaking about a half mile out in the Pacific in front of huge, house-size rocks bordering the entrance to Pillar Point Harbor, the waves at Mavs are truly deadly. The spot doesn't even really break until it's over ten feet, and from there, it pushes the limits of rideability with 30-foot-plus leviathans capping the outside reefs. In addition to this outside zone, there are two other take-off spots: The Corner where the majority of riders sit and Lates Bowl, another peak south that catches sets swinging outside the main take-off zone. Unlike other big-wave locales, which feature a large drop followed by a mushy shoulder, on prime northwest swells Mavericks is a freight-train right boasting enormous walled-up lines that throw out gaping top-to-bottom tubes even when it's huge.

With such an intense atmosphere, one false move can cause waveriders to be pinned to the bottom, broken apart by huge rocks on the inside, or knocked unconscious by the force of the wave. This is as dangerous as it gets, folks, so do not under any circumstances attempt this spot unless you have many years of experience in heavy surf over 20 feet. And even then, you still aren't safe.

Though Mavericks is generally ridden by experts only, it's such a powerful spot, even the top guns can fall victim to its ferocity. In 1994, Hawaiian big-wave charger Mark Foo drowned after falling mid-face on a drop into a medium-size 15 footer. This catapulted the sport into the mainstream media, and although this wasn't the first death in big surf and certainly not the last, all the attention on Foo's death at Mavericks has given big-wave surfing a much more menacing countenance. Now, the search is on to find even more breaks with such dangerous qualities, and the world's heavy-water crew have located several in the past few years, including one in South Africa and one on an isolated reef off California. Like any extreme sport, riding large surf at Mavs is appealing for its adrenaline-pumping danger, but as Foo said himself, "If you want the ultimate thrill, you've got to be willing to pay the ultimate price."

Above left: *Even with all of its menacing conditions, Mavericks still remains a beautiful spot when the conditions come together.*

Above: *It's either your worst nightmare or your most intense thrill. Mid-face at Mavericks.*

Left: *With huge, cold faces like this, it's easy to see why many have labeled Mavericks as surfing's Mt. Everest.*

RINCON, CALIFORNIA

California's Rincon del Mar is known as the "Queen of the Coast" for good reason. When this classic right-hand pointbreak turns on, its machine-like perfection can rival some of the best spots in the world. One look at Rincon when it's wrapped tight with pinwheeling lines of swell, and you'll understand just how truly epic the Golden State's waves can get. During days like this, the fabled point peels with perfect precision for over 300 yards—from the outside reef through the inside cove—offering surfers one of the best pointbreak experiences on North America's West Coast.

Because the point is within sight of Highway 101 just south of Carpinteria, many car accidents have been narrowly avoided by distracted surfers driving along the coast catching a glimpse of waves hitting Rincon's cobblestone-lined cove. The place breaks best in the winter on head-high or bigger north and west swells, and the lineup is divided into three distinct take-off zones: Indicator, the Rivermouth, and the Cove. Approaching waves first hit the zone farthest north— Indicator. Here, slower rights form far outside the point and start bending inside toward the highway. Next down the line is the hollow section known as the Rivermouth for its proximity to Rincon Creek's ocean entrance. From this area, the wave curves into the Cove, which is the most popular and crowded of the three peaks. The Cove's waves reel from just inside the bay all the way down the beach to the dangerous boulders bordering the road. On most days, each zone makes up its own little surf spot, but on perfect swells, the three connect up, and amazing rides can be lined up from Indicator all the way through the Cove to the freeway.

Because Rincon's waves get so good and are so visible to the highway, count on major crowds on the best days. People from up and down the coast, including the world's top pros, head for the 'Con when it fires. But with the three breaks dividing up the point, you can usually find an empty shoulder if you look hard enough. And if you're into sizeable waves, Rincon can handle some of the biggest surf Southern California has to offer. The break retains its pointbreak symmetry up to twelve or fifteen feet when nearby beaches are closing down under the heavy swell. But regardless of whether you catch it big or small, crowded or not, no California surf trip is complete without visiting the Queen and viewing her magnificence first-hand. Catch her on a good day, and she'll leave you feeling like surfing royalty.

Right: *The Queen of the Coast displaying her crown jewels.*

RUGGLES, RHODE ISLAND

Although the U.S. East Coast isn't usually regarded for the size of its surf, Ruggles is the one true big-wave Mecca to be found on America's right coast. Once regarded as a semi-secret spot among the notoriously tight-lipped New Englanders, a series of magazine features in the early '90s revealed this perfect right point reeling off with 15- to 18-foot perfection, and Ruggles gained the label as the East Coast's premier big-wave break. Soon after, the surfing masses began descending on the sleepy little town of Newport, Rhode Island.

Located in a ritzy section of the city where mansions dot the rustic New England seascape, the break is named for Ruggles Avenue, which runs right up to the beachside bluff overlooking the lineup. The spot itself is situated in front of this cliffside vista, bordered on both sides by small bays. Although most of the photos focus on the right point and its massive, watery shoulders, there are actually several other spots around the craggy bluff.

Just off the headland, the wave is split into a big peak, holding both rights and lefts. The "Lefts off the Point," as they're called by locals, offer an excellent left-hand pointbreak setup capable of producing up to 200-yard-long, barreling zippers. The Rights off the Point or simply, The Point, is a huge, often fat right-hander that produces large, walled-up faces that bend in toward the main take-off zone, known as The Channel. Here the waves gain more power and become better organized as they move into the shallower water of the bay. This section is what most of the photos show, and it's truly an epic wave able to handle whatever size swell the Atlantic can muster. Locals have reported it to break up to twenty-five feet in face height, throwing out high-pocket barrels and offering rides up to 150 yards long. Continuing on down the line, there's Around the Corner, which is the break's end section, and it can produce huge square pits as it peels off toward one of Newport's other spots, First Beach. The three rights don't usually link up all the way through, except on rare occasions when all the conditions come together just right, but either section, especially when it's big, is exceptional in and of itself.

Although Ruggles is primarily known as a big-wave spot, it'll work from chest-high and up. In order for the place to break like it's shown in the photos, there needs to be a massive storm system spinning off large south-southeast groundswells. This occurs most often from a hurricane, so late summer, particularly September, is when Ruggles is most likely to show its true big-wave magnificence. Unfortunately, like most East Coast breaks, this doesn't occur very often, so don't expect to just drop by and luck into macking 20-foot surf. True big-wave conditions happen very infrequently— probably fewer than ten times a year—so keep a close eye on the weather and establish a connection with a dialed-in local to get the goods at Ruggles. Like most other big-wave locales, the crew here is very close-knit. Suffering through brutal winters requiring fullsuits, booties, hoods, and gloves, as well as lengthy flat spells, these locals deserve—and will take—the best sets on the best days. But with such heavy conditions, a crushing inside breaking onto huge rocks, and relatively cold water year-round, Ruggles is one East Coast spot that can take care of itself.

Above: *Ruggles flexes its big-wave muscles.*

Right: *Jeremy Saukel projecting across a mid-sized Ruggles wall.*

SEBASTIAN INLET, FLORIDA

Named for third-century Christian martyr Saint Sebastian, this central Florida surfbreak is viewed with almost holy reverence by East Coast waveriders. Built in the late 1960s, the man-made inlet's curved jetty produces some of the most consistent, well-shaped, and highly photographed waves on the entire U.S. eastern seaboard. These prime conditions attract thousands of surfers, and the spot hosts numerous amateur and professional surf contests, arguably making Sebastian Inlet the epicenter of East Coast surfing.

Located roughly 16 miles south of Melbourne Beach, Sebastian is broken into three breaks—First Peak, Second Peak, and Third Peak—based on their proximity to the Inlet. The star attraction is First Peak, a wedging right located directly next to the rocks. Here, waves are given a boost in size and strength from the jetty's swell refraction, and will usually be a foot bigger and more hollow than anywhere in the immediate area. The peak is an intense bowling right-hander featuring frequent barrels upon take-off followed by a racetrack section with ample room for big carves and high-flying aerials. These great waves have big appeal, and several of the planet's top surfers live nearby, including six-time World Champion Kelly Slater and 2001 Champion C.J. Hobgood, so unless you're an expert surfer or known local, it's unlikely you'll break into First Peak's well-established pecking order, and you're better off starting a little farther down the beach.

About 20 yards north, you'll find Second Peak and beyond that, Third Peak. These spots don't have the size or consistency of First Peak but still possess quite a bit of power. Both waves offer steep rights and lefts, with the left-handers becoming particularly favorable on swells with any hint of a north angle. These two are also less crowded, but on good days, the entire beach can become mobbed with hundreds of people, clogging the lineup with all manner of equipment and experience levels. And outside of the human flotsam, expect to share the waves with another crowd—sharks. With Florida the shark attack capital of the world, Sebastian Inlet is almost as famous for its predatory fish population as its quality surf. Sighting and attacks are frequent—averaging roughly two or three bites a year—but these incidents are usually fairly benign, involving only minor cuts and scrapes. Plus, with so many other people in the water, your odds of getting nipped are dramatically decreased.

Although most of central Florida is well developed, Sebastian Inlet is fairly remote. However, because the area is within a state park, access and facilities are excellent. The park is one of the state's most visited and offers well-maintained bathrooms, showers, and picnic pavilions. Also available are campsites, a snack bar, a gift shop, and a bait shop. Both the park and the waves are most popular during the summer, when warm, trunkable water attracts tourists and hurricanes produce the best southeast-east swells. With such top-notch waves, surfers, and amenities, Sebastian Inlet is among the most sacred of East Coast surf spots.

Above: *After years of experience, the best surfers instinctively know when First Peak is about to open wide. Charlie Kuhn prepares to be enveloped.*

Right, inset: *With plenty of ramps for boosting, Sebastian Inlet has always been one of the leading lineups for aerial exploration. Eric Taylor taking flight at Second Peak.*

Right: *Local Bill Hartley and First Peak's wedging bowl have developed a deep relationship over the years.*

SOUPBOWL, BATHSHEBA, BARBADOS

The easternmost of the Caribbean Sea's Windward Islands, Barbados, offers a wide variety of waveriding opportunities for surfers seeking everything from dangerously thick barrels above urchin-encrusted reefs to gentle lines peeling along cotton-white beaches. Seated roughly a hundred miles south of Hurricane Alley—the track Atlantic tropical systems follow—Soupbowl, located in the East Coast town of Bathsheba, is the boss dog of Barbados surfing. Despite the idyllic backdrops and the serene ambiance that characterizes life in Bathsheba, it typically attracts a reckless and hard-core surfing breed.

Every year, hundreds of surfers, both professional and amateur, frequent Soupbowl for its consistent power, the utter rippability of its many hollow sections, and the photogenic quality of the spot itself. Best during the swell-endowed months of the Northern Hemisphere's fall and early winter, Soupbowl is often thought to be a perpetually onshore spot. Contrary to that reputation, though, the break does enjoy offshore conditions more than a dozen times a year in spite of vulnerability to consistent easterly tradewinds. The wave works best on a north swell from head-high up, closing out after ten feet. It begins as a jacking wedge before it drops out below sea-level, offering an eerily perfect tube section. It then bowls down the line in a series of hollow pockets and smackable glory sections. On smaller swells, there is also a shorter left that bends into shallower water, offering a quick tube followed by a launch ramp perfectly suited for aerial maneuvers. An added attraction to Soupbowl in recent years is the Independence Day Pro, a heavily attended professional surfing contest held every November.

Barbados's breaks aren't by any means empty. Soupbowl in particular has the reputation of becoming extremely congested at weekends and during afternoon glassoffs, when packs of surfers from the other coasts wind down from their workdays with sessions. However, Parlour and High Rock—two deepwater reefbreaks located just south of the break—serve as overflow when the Bowl is pushing maximum density.

Above: *Soupbowl, Barbados' premier wave, serves up punchy reefbreak thrills amidst a vibrant and laid back Caribbean culture.*

Besides the crowds, the reefs have proven to be extremely debilitating to the visiting surfer, and any cuts should be treated immediately to avoid contracting staph and other bacterial infections. Sea urchins are a daily nuisance, and caution should be taken when walking in from or out to lineups. Man-o'-war, barracuda, and mosquitoes are other threats to be on the lookout for. But for every urchin spine suffered, there's a barrel savored. For every ocean thrashing, there's a crisp rail dance to a foamy shoulder. For every bug bite endured, there's an azure lip line awaiting your bash. Overall, the friendly demeanor of the Bathsheba locals combined with the prehistoric setting and consistent, shockingly punchy waves will continue to make Soupbowl a key traveling destination for surfers for decades to come.

Below: *While onshore trades are common at Soupbowl, when the winds do turn offshore, the results can be spectacular.*

STEAMER LANE, SANTA CRUZ, CALIFORNIA

Known as California's northern "Surf City," Santa Cruz is one of the Golden State's hotbeds for both epic waves and incredible surfing talent. Facing south, the city picks up heaps of swell from almost all directions, and the locale's numerous points, reefs, and beaches focus the wave energy into several world-class breaks. These stellar conditions breed amazing surfers, and Santa Cruz is home to several of the best aerialists and big-wave riders on the planet. Although there are numerous and even better breaks in Santa Cruz, the town's major arena for waves and the place where all Santa Cruz locals must prove themselves is Steamer Lane.

Part of the reason Steamers is such a showplace for surfing is its setting. The spot's four peaks all break at the bottom of huge cliffs, which are bordered with walkways and handrails for easy viewing of the action below. Crowds of people line these cliffs during good swells, making the Lane a veritable theater, encouraging surfers to raise the performance level to a pinnacle.

The first of the four peaks is located directly at the bottom of the cliff topped with the lighthouse and surf museum, and it's called The Point. The Point is a right-hand, rock pointbreak, and this is where some of the hottest high-performance surfing goes down with the top surfers jockeying for position in the tight take-off zone next to the rocks. Farther down the cove from The Point lies The Slot. This is another right peak that serves as an overflow zone for The Point's bigger sets or sometimes as an inside break for the next spot, Middle Peak. Middle Peak is a big A-frame located center stage at Steamers. It offers both lefts and rights with the lefts being a little more hollow. This peak is also the focus on the bigger days, when the largest Pacific swells march in and unload on the Lane's outer reefs. Lastly, there's Indicator. This peak is a long, hollow right point inside of Middle Peak. Indicator catches some of Middle's waves, which wash through, and it's where most of the beginners and groms hang out.

On most days, the Lane will be totally zooed out with hundreds of surfers on all types of equipment. For years, the Santa Cruz locals have attempted to regulate the packed lineup with strict pecking orders, threats, and sometimes even violence, but there are

simply too many people out for even the burliest of locals to handle. Avoid congested times like weekends or school holidays if you want to score a few waves to yourself. The Lane's water is cold all year-round, but California's temperate climate keeps things fairly mild, so a ⅘ with booties will carry you through even the coldest months. Since the beach faces south, the waves can get good any time of year: stormy winter surf from the north is cleaned up as it wraps around Santa Cruz's protective headlands, and big summer souths push directly into the town's window. In addition to the great surf, Steamer Lane gained international attention in the '80s when the Association of Surfing Professional's O'Neill Coldwater Classic began holding annual professional surf competitions here. Since the contest started, locals have surfed competitively against several of the top surfers in the world, and often, the Santa Cruz surfers beat the visitors. Today, with a new pool of talent that's blowing up faster than ever, the Lane is recognized as one of the most innovative surf towns, providing ample evidence to support the Surf City namesake.

Above: *With all its rocky nooks and crannies, it's no wonder Steamer Lane boasts so many great setups.*

Right: *When the swell gets big, Middle Peak is Steamer Lane's main attraction. Unidentified surfer nabs a nice one from the crowd.*

TRES PALMAS, PUERTO RICO

The Caribbean isle of Puerto Rico has often been compared to Hawaii for its many powerful reefbreaks, and one of its most famous spots, Tres Palmas, can do a really good imitation of Sunset Beach when it gets big. Named for three palm trees growing in front of the lineup, Tres Palmas is located on the island's northwest coast, near the town of Rincon. The spot is legendary for holding macking swells up to 25 feet, making it one of Puerto Rico's premier big-wave surfbreaks.

The coast around Rincon faces west toward the Mona Passage, which separates the island from the Dominican Republic. Because of its location, the town is in prime position to funnel in large northwest swells and also reap offshore winds from the regular east-northeast trades. The ideal storm for Tres Palmas occurs when a large, wintertime frontal system closely hugs the U.S. seaboard as it makes its way toward the North Atlantic. Although it will break from around four feet and up, the most sought-after conditions occur when these fronts send bombing swells over eight feet toward the spot's waiting Elkhorn coral reef. The wave itself is a long, right-hand wall rideable for almost 200 yards with three peaks along its length: one to the north, one in the middle, and one on the south end. The middle peak is the primary take-off zone and can get packed with a hard-core group of locals and expatriate Americans with the other two peaks acting as overflow zones as crowds get thick. Even though the wave is big, it's not really top-to-bottom, so it doesn't get as heavy as other breaks of similar size. Instead, Tres Palmas throws out rifling high-pocket barrels, and small-wave maneuvers such as cutbacks and off-the-tops are possible even at top sizes. Take a beefy board around 7 feet 2 inches to 7 foot 6 inches for when it's up to 15 feet, and then go for a real gun on the biggest days.

Puerto Rico is a U.S. territory, so the country is easy to access and get around. But the island is also well known for its high crime rate, so exercise caution in the bigger cities like San Juan. Rincon is the busiest surfing area in the country, which means it has many accommodation options and surf shops. The water is crystal clear, warm, and trunkable year-round. With the teeming Elkhorn coral, sea fans, and other marine life growing below, it'll feel like you're surfing over a living organism. The break and its beautiful setting are so near to surfers' hearts, that when development threatened to destroy it in the early part of the new millennium, activist groups such as Surfrider Foundation and Surfer's Environmental Alliance fought and won a heated political battle to save the spot. Plans are now under way to declare the region a protected National Maritime Preserve, which would guarantee that the beautiful island lineup remains pure and pristine for many years to come.

Above: *Navigating the inside bowl at Tres Palmas.*

Left: *The palm trees at Tres Palmas provide much-needed shade for wave watchers.*

Below: *As one of the most beautiful Caribbean breaks, it's no wonder surfers have fought hard to protect the environmental sanctity of Puerto Rico's Tres Palmas.*

CENTRAL AMERICA

Since the mid-1960s, masses of Californian surfers have ventured south of the Mexican border in search of waves. Heading down the dusty desert roads of Baja's narrow peninsula and eventually into the more populated regions along the Mex's mainland coast, waveriders discovered a gateway to a seemingly endless array of new surfbreaks. But the southerly migration didn't end there. In the following years, waveriders from all over lit out deeper into Central America, uncovering amazing, uncrowded lineups stretching down to Panama's border with Colombia. These days, Mexico and Central America are among the most-often visited surf destinations in the world. In particular, places like Cabo San Lucas and Costa Rica have become favorites among travelers seeking quick, easy, and relatively inexpensive international destinations. But even though some of these spots have become a bit passé in the world of hard-core surfaris, countless less-explored and more challenging lineups lie waiting in nearby countries such as Nicaragua. Whether you're seeking a relatively painless first surf trip or looking for something way more adventurous, Mexico and Central America have something to satisfy almost every type of surf traveler.

Right: *Pacific pulse at Pavones.*

KILLERS, ISLAS DE TODOS SANTOS, BAJA MEXICO

When the Windansea Surf Club first ventured out to Baja Mexico's Islas de Todos Santos in the mid-'60s, it didn't have the proper equipment or the knowledge to ride the place successfully. Today, thanks to a handful of brave Californians led by Mike "Snips" Parsons—the undisputed king of Todos—it retains its reputation as one of the scariest waves in the world, with a cold, open-ocean environment less inviting than Oahu's Waimea Bay, which, until the mid-'90s, was still the undisputed king of big-wave spots.

Killers is located on the northwest side of the northernmost of Todos Santos's two islands, 12 miles off the coast of Ensenada. Easily one of the top three biggest paddle-in waves in the world, this break has provided a big-wave training ground for many surfers, especially Californians taking the boat ride from Ensenada. When it's cranking, Killers is a wave for experienced big-wave surfers only. Breaking in very deep water over huge boulders, it gets quite turbulent. The boulders create giant boils in the face, nightmare rips, and even whirlpools underwater.

Killers works best on big northwest swells, more common in the Northern Hemisphere winter, and the more west the better. Too much north in a swell makes for fewer hairball drops and a mushier wave in general. The big boils churning near a natural fixture composed of the same large boulders marks the take-off spot. The wave forms a big ledge that a rider must stroke with everything he's got to make it over. Many times that means paddling deeper toward those ominous boils. Getting caught inside here can be hellacious, as a treacherous rip sweeps the surfer toward a rocky cliff beyond the impact zone.

Todos will usually be twice as big as anything on the west coast's mainland, and a big-wave rhino chaser is the only surfboard one should even think about using here. The board should also have a little extra thickness to deal with the debilitating foam and chop. A fullsuit is needed all year and booties are a good idea in the winter.

Like most heavy-water spots, Killers requires commitment, experience, and respect. But unlike many big-wave spots, such as Waimea and Mavericks, it also breaks small and can be ridden down to five or six feet, and it can get fairly rippable. It's then that a shorter board will work.

Despite dropping slightly in popularity over the past decade, partly due to increased attention on the tow-in phenomenon, Killers reestablished itself on the big-wave radar in 1998 when Taylor Knox rode the biggest wave of the year at the Reef Big Wave World Championships, earning $50,000 from the K2 Challenge. This just goes to show that even though it might fall asleep for a while, when Killers really happens, the whole world takes notice.

Above: *An aerial view of the lineup at Killers, on Mexico's Islas de Todos Santos. This wave still stands as one of the top three most challenging big-wave locales in the world.*

Right: *Southern California hellman Evan Slater takes it steep and deep at Killers. The wave is as deadly as its name suggests.*

OPEN DOORS, ISLA NATIVIDAD, BAJA MEXICO

Isla Natividad is located a short plane ride off the central coast of the Baja Peninsula. Although many of this tiny island's in-your-face beachbreaks resemble each other, Open Doors is the most well known. Surfers have ventured here since the '60s, but the island didn't receive much attention until the '80s, when the increasing Southern California crowds drove more and more surfers south of the border. Today, Natividad still remains one of the most rugged trips one can take. If you enjoy camping on a dusty, barren stretch of beach, observing the slow pace of birds, rodents, and sea life and have absolutely nothing to do but surf, this may be your heaven on earth.

Like most breaks on the island, Open Doors is marked by extreme inconsistency, since the channel between Natividad and Punta Eugenia saps most swells' power. In order to reach its potential, Open Doors requires a solid south swell to hit the southernmost point of the island. Then it becomes a barrel-fest of epic proportions—left barrels spitting two or three times, right barrels wrapping clear around the east side of the point, split-peak barrels mirroring each bowl's activity. Like many beachbreaks, this spot thumps only a few strokes from the beach and can hold size up to double-overhead or bigger. During punchier swells, this wave has been known to break as many surfboards as Puerto Escondido. As tides shift with the swell's oscillating pulse, this place can go from sucking sand off the bottom and coughing it out in a flume of spit to laying off and allowing for a few maneuvers on the face. Conditions can switch from fast, furious, and hollow to fun, friendly, and rippable in the blink of an eye.

Facing southeast, all-day offshores are not unusual here. Sometimes, though, the wind can blow a little too hard, spelling disaster on smaller swells. Crowds are rarely a problem, and empty lineups are common, even today. While the peak of hurricane season—summer to early fall—is typically the best time to catch prime Southern Hemis with nicely shaved sandbars, Open Doors works between April and December, too. A fullsuit is usually needed year-round, as the chilly California current lies just offshore.

As for hazards, forget about it. If you make landfall after the convulsing, life-flashing flight from Ensenada, you've survived the worst of it. Go for broke! One final plus to this extremely fickle wave is its photogenic potential—crystal-clear water, perpetually front-lit, and only a short tumble to the beach. Open Doors is one of the best setups in the world for photos, if you're into that sort of thing.

Above: *Why in the world these guys are still on the beach remains a mystery. On the notoriously boring sands of Isla Natividad, it's either surfing, sleeping, or taking in the sun.*

Right: *Open Doors, Isla Natividad's best-known spot, can be one of the most photogenic surfbreaks on earth, making it a favorite weekend trip for California pros and photographers.*

PAVONES, COSTA RICA

"Imagine hitting a baseball 450 feet over the center field wall and into the seats. Imagine the sensation of the bat striking the ball. Imagine that sensation lasting one minute."

Taken from the book *In Search of Captain Zero*, this quote is surf scribe Allan Weisbecker's description of the incredible left pointbreak waves of Costa Rica's Pavones. In a country filled with hundreds of points, this jungle spot is among the finest in Costa and for that matter, the world. Situated along the shores of El Rio Claro, Pavones' legendary lefts reel at a lightning-quick pace from the rivermouth down the cobblestone and palm tree-lined point, finally exhausting themselves in a sheltered cove almost a mile inside the bay. Connecting the wave from beginning to end will test the limits of speed and endurance, while blowing the minds of even the most road-tested surf travelers.

This dream wave is located in the far southern region of Costa Rica near the border of Panama inside Golfo Dulce. Because the spot is in such a sheltered location, it breaks only on large southwest swells, but during the rainy season from April to October, these types of conditions occur nearly every week. You'll know Pavones is firing when the breaks to the north start closing out with the arrival of huge south swells. That's when it's time to jump in the car and zip south down the Pan American Highway toward the border. The ride from Jaco is around ten hours, but when Pavones turns on and connects all the way through, it's well worth the drive.

Located inside thick rain forest, the area immediately surrounding the lineup used to be fairly desolate, but due to word of mouth in the waveriding community, locals and expatriate Americans have built up the jungle point to take advantage of the thousands of surf tourists who visit every year. Now there are plenty of small cabins in which to stay the night, or you can camp on the beach if you prefer. Unfortunately, because modern wave-forecasting technology makes it easy to predict the coming swells, it's not unlikely to have almost a hundred people converge on this little outpost at once. But thankfully,

because the break stretches for so long a distance, there is plenty of room to spread out. On average-size swells, the wave breaks for a few hundred yards and closes out before reforming down farther inside the point. This process repeats itself over and over, forming three or four distinct sections. But when a perfectly angled, large southwest strikes the coast and the tide and other conditions are just right, the sections disappear and rides of up to a thousand yards are possible. Snag one of these waves from the river to the inside bay, and Pavones will provide you with an experience just like Weisbecker describes.

Above: *On a solid south swell like this, Pavones can peel for nearly a mile. Jason Borte gearing up for a leg-burner.*

Left: *Welcome to the jungle. Pavones.*

Below: *Jeremy Saukel downshifts on the inside racetrack at Pavones.*

PLAYA ESCONDIDA, JACO, COSTA RICA

The English translation of "Costa Rica" is "Rich Coast," and this title holds especially true for traveling surfers who'll find an abundance of watery treasures along the country's numerous points, reefs, and beaches. Although there are ample waves up and down both seaboards, the Central Pacific towns of Jaco and Hermosa are Costa's surfing headquarters. This area is generally the first stop-off for many of the country's numerous surf tourists, and it contains the largest concentration of surf-related businesses as well. There are numerous great breaks along this stretch of shore, including Hermosa's thumping beachbreak barrels, Roca Loca's perilous rocky reefs, and Jaco's many mellow peaks, but the area's most world-class setup exists just north of Jaco's tourist strip near the little village of Herradura. Just offshore from this fishing town lies the reefbreak known as Playa Escondida.

Located in front of a rock point jutting around thirty yards into the ocean, this horseshoe-shaped wave tightly focuses the raw ocean power into a single A-frame peak. There's both a right and left that spin ruler-edged lines down the length of the rocky outcropping, providing intense, barrel-laden rides especially on the lefts. Escondida will work from chest-high and up, but anything bigger than a couple of feet overhead and the place gets heavy. With an unforgiving rock reef just a few feet below the surface and large rocks lining the inside that are rumored to have disemboweled at least one unlucky soul, swells with any serious size are best left to the more experienced. As Escondida is located only a short distance from the popular town of Jaco, you can count on there being more than a few surfers who'll take the challenge. On days with any hint of swell, plan on sharing the lineup with a fairly thick crowd. And because Escondida's take-off zone

fits only a handful of people, with two riders per wave maximum, expect plenty of hassling and jockeying for set waves.

The water in Costa Rica is extremely warm year-round, so boardies, lots of sunblock, and a rashguard are all you'll need through every season. The wet season, from April to October, will feature the biggest and most consistent waves as southwest swells pump near continuous surf all along the country's Pacific coastline. However, the dry season, during November through March, still gets regular surf with some sizeable days, too. And because the majority of surfers travel here in the summer months, this off-season also holds the additional allure of being the least crowded. But no matter when you visit, make sure you hit Escondida at least once, because Costa Rica is indeed rich with surf and Playa Escondida is one of her crown jewels.

Left: *It costs around $10 a head for a boat out to Escondida, but judging by this shot of Bill Hartley, it's worth every penny.*

Below: *Bill Hartley deep inside a throaty Playa Escondida left.*

PUERTO ESCONDIDO, OAXACA, MEXICO

Puerto Escondido is without a doubt the biggest, nastiest, most ferocious beachbreak in the history of the sport, responsible for more surfboard carnage than any other single spot in the world. Located in the state of Oaxaca, this filthy, belching beast of a wave constantly ups the ante for prospective players. Although many places in the world employ the moniker "The (insert locale) Pipeline," nowhere is that qualifier more fitting than here, at the Mexican Pipeline.

A deep, underwater canyon just offshore of the break sucks in all the energy from south swells and focuses it onto the sandbars of Zicatela, creating sandy leviathans that are the stuff nightmares are made of. Breaking so unsettlingly close to shore, Puerto's unpredictable rips can take a surfer places he doesn't want to go—like right in the middle of an impact zone with a 20-foot A-frame preparing to unload overhead. Everything should be timed right—from paddle-out to take-off. The most important rule to surfing big Puerto—next to showing up with the proper equipment—is once you're going . . . go! Pulling back here can be the worst mistake you'll ever make, and possibly the last one, too. And although it seems like the loudest, darkest, and scariest place, the tube is always the safest place to be.

The Northern Hemisphere summer is the best time to hit Puerto, when the winds are more likely to be offshore in the mornings and afternoons. This being the rainy season, sandbars are also best at this time, creating classic Escondido slabs rideable well past triple-overhead. Winter west swells are typically smaller and less consistent. But when they do make it to the shore, the waves can get very good, though they are generally smaller, more manageable, and less scary. Puerto Escondido often blows out by eleven in the morning, allowing surfers plenty of siesta time in-between thrashings.

You will break some, if not all, of your surfboards during any given excursion here. Boards for peak-season Puerto should be guns—straight pintails with extra-heavy glass and narrow enough for speed and stability in the pit. In the winter, hot-dog boards might be ridden with some regularity, but even then you will probably break

them. Helmets might keep you from suffering a concussion from your board, but they won't keep the sandbar from snapping your neck.

Puerto Escondido and its surrounding breaks have been key surfing destinations since the '60s and '70s, but the place used to be much more difficult to get to. Now, there's an airport close by that functions as a conveyor belt for surfers, increasing the number of Puerto frequenters tenfold. And at a wide-open thumping beachbreak like this, that many boards and bodies floating around can be disastrous. But since it's such a shifty and unpredictable beachbreak, the fear factor of Puerto Escondido's waves transcends everything else. After all, you can do everything right and still get drilled. This place is, quite simply, too intense for even localism.

Above: *Even on smaller days, Puerto Escondido can still give your board and body a thrashing. The barrel rides, more often than not, are well worth it.*
Right: *Two surfers split the power at Puerto Escondido, the world's heaviest beachbreak.*

SALSA BRAVA, PUERTO VIEJO, COSTA RICA

As more of its treasures were exposed to the world throughout the '80s, Costa Rica steadily grew as a major surf destination with its diversity of breaks, stable government, and exposure to two different oceans' swells. Yet while there are far more spots on the Pacific side of the country—including world-class points, horseshoe-shaped reefs, and hollow rivermouths—Costa Rica's biggest and most bloodthirsty wave lies on the Caribbean coast about 50 miles south of the port city of Limon, in the town of Puerto Viejo. Quite simply, Salsa Brava—translating to "angry sauce" in Spanish—is a furious wave. It's a lightning-fast right-hander pitching a few feet from punji-stake coral. And although Costa Rica may indeed be a great first-time surf trip, and a safe destination in general, this wave is far from harmless.

At its best—west wind grooming a short-interval, southeasterly swell—Salsa jacks up on a shallow patch of reef called First Peak. This section has a thin and closely guarded take-off zone that can leave you soaking on your board or force you to settle for the left—a short but zippy tube. However, snagging a good right here can lead you to the roundest, most top-to-bottom cavern you've ever seen. Down the line waits Second Peak, which more agile surfers often connect from First Peak—backdooring it all the way through. To navigate Salsa successfully, a surfer must commit to its insides. The barrel is what makes this warped thing a surf spot. When it's cranking, Salsa allows for very few turns, and attempting to downshift might leave you stranded in the impact zone—somewhere you don't want to be. After all, people have died on these reefs. The wave can hold size well past double-overhead, and if horribly shallow Salsa Brava at that size doesn't scare you, it's doubtful anything in Costa Rica will. Your fastest stick is the only option here when it's going off, and with the water tropically delicious all year around, a wetsuit is totally unnecessary. Wearing a helmet isn't a bad idea, though. You'll probably see more than one guy out wearing one, indicative of just how treacherous the reef is there. Also, be very careful when stroking through the serpentine maze of channels. If possible, wait and follow a local. You

can bet there will be plenty of them paddling out when Salsa's doing its thing.

While the Northern Hemisphere summer is the best time for surf on the Pacific side with frequent rains bettering the often walled-up sandbars, it's pretty much always the wet season on the Caribbean coast, and it can pour for days on end. The winter is the time to be here, though, with better-directed energy more likely, although storm-driven winds can quickly ruin an otherwise good swell. If you have the country wired, as many Americans do, you can time the Costa season perfectly—winter on the Caribbean and summer on the Pacific. But after being ejected from one of Salsa Brava's once-in-a-lifetime, below-sea-level grinders, you may never want to surf any other spot again, and if you get dragged along the cheese-grater reef, you might never be able to.

Above: Right where you don't want to be—caught inside at Salsa Brava.
Right: The tube is actually the safest place to be on a bloodthirsty wave like Salsa Brava.

STAIRWAYS, RIVAS PROVINCE, NICARAGUA

Before you embark on a surf trip you have to ask yourself, "What am I looking for?" Most people just want the basics—no crowds; good probability of scoring; never under chest-high and averaging a few feet overhead; offshore all the time; world-class points and reefbreaks, but some fun bustable beachies, too; and always-warm water. All this and more can be found in Nicaragua—a land of question marks, a land of exclamation points (and reefs and coves . . .)

Surfbreak-wise, Nicaragua is generally thought of as being similar to Costa Rica, but without the crowds. Most spots receive plenty of southerly groundswells during the Northern Hemisphere winter, but the rest of the year is fairly consistent as well, and like Costa Rica, there are also two coasts to choose from in Nicaragua. The southwestern province of Rivas, which is the capital city, lies on the southwestern side of the country on a narrow strip of land between the Pacific Ocean and Lake Nicaragua. Rivas is where most of the better-known spots are, but there are plenty of others that beckon surfers with empty lineups. The winds are almost always offshore here thanks to consistent easterly trades blowing over the expansive lake. One of the best waves in the Rivas Province is Stairways, a fast left-hand reef-point. Stairways breaks a few coves up from Playa Gigante in front of a small restaurant/hotel. The wave here starts as a bowly peak that jacks up suddenly—a total surprise—and makes the take-off twice as critical. No mistakes can be made here, as it is the most shallow part of the ride. Several surfers have left skin here, just by barely grazing the bottom. The reef is razor coral, as sharp as reefs come. If you make the drop, though, you're in for a deep tube followed by a long, sectiony wall perfect for lip smacks and fading rail turns. The wave then might throw another tube at the end or provide a big mound to smash. Stairways is an excellent wave when it's on, but it needs a good-size swell to break. It also gets creepily shallow at low tide here, so it's best to limit your sessions to mid-tide.

The coast is rugged, some spots are hard to get to, and the mosquitoes carry malaria and dengue. But all in all Nicaragua is

probably the most low-maintenance and ultimately satisfying surf trip you can take.

Above: *A breathtaking Nicaraguan sunset, and almost no surfers to share the beauty with. Ah, paradise.*

Right: *North Carolina goofyfoot Dylan Stone, locked and loaded over viciously sharp coral at Stairways, Nicaragua.*

Above Right: *"Anybody seen my sunscreen?" A trio of traveling American surfers gear up before hitting the waves in Nicaragua. The surf trip remains the most romanticized aspect of waveriding.*

WITCHES ROCK, SANTA ROSA NATIONAL PARK, COSTA RICA

Compared with the central and southern regions of the country, the northwestern beaches of Costa Rica's Pacific side are much better suited for the country's dry season from November through March. While the summertime wet season sees loads of powerful southwest swells firing in the more southerly areas, the coastline in the Guanacaste province from Playa Negra north to the Nicaraguan border gets most of its best swells from winter storms that pump in regular waves from the northwest and west. One of the more remote, yet scenic surf venues in this part of the country is the legendary beachbreak known as Witches Rock.

Located a short distance from Nicaragua inside Santa Rosa National Park, Witches Rock, or Roca Bruja in Spanish, is named for a towering volcanic rock that sits just beyond the lineup. The massive boulder has an odd, tapered shape with many crevices and holes that emit an otherworldly noise when the wind and waves careen off their surfaces, inspiring locals to give it its witchy moniker. But outside of its appearance and sounds, the rock's interruption of sand flow also helps mold the area's waves from shut-down closeouts into reeling beachbreak barrels. Witches is a powerful A-frame that favors rights, but it can get just as intense lefts. The wave is walled up, extremely fast, and the hard winter offshores—called Papagayos—groom the surf into meaty, board-breaking tubes. It'll work from two to ten feet, getting really powerful when it's big. Although the bottom is sand, the impact zone can administer rough poundings, but because the surf zone is small and breaking only in the shadow of the rock, an easier paddle-out can often be found by walking just beyond the lineup in either direction. Roca Bruja favors higher tides, as dead low tends to make the wave close out more. Also, because it's in a remote area, crowds are thinner than other spots, but occasionally, boatloads of people can invade the break during predictable swells.

To reach Witches Rock, you can either drive in with a 4x4 from the National Park entrance or rent a boat in nearby Play Del Coco. Each way has its downsides. The drive involves a mile-long walk to reach the lineup and can be inaccessible during heavy rains, whereas the boat is expensive, running about $200. Make sure you bring everything you need, including water, food, and sunscreen, because the beach here is totally desolate with no facilities at all. You won't ever need more than boardshorts for the water temperatures, but when the wind really blows a light wetsuit vest is a welcome accessory. Camping at the spot is possible, but you'll be roughing it, so pitch a tent only if you like a really bare-bones experience. Nevertheless, despite its remote location, Witches Rock remains one of the top spots in Guanacaste and it offers truly supernatural waves.

Above: *Jeff Myers with a little aerial magic at Witches Rock.*

Right: *You know a wave is fast when it's already feathering up 20-yards ahead of the curl. Supernatural speed is common at Witches Rock.*